CAN PARLIAMENT TAKE

CW00342911

Funded by the Joseph Rowntree Reform Trust.

The Joseph Rowntree Reform Trust has supported this
work in recognition of the importance of the issue. The
facts presented and the views expressed in this report are,
however, those of the authors and not necessarily those
of the Trust. www.jrrt.org.uk

Nick Harvey

Served as MP for North Devon (1992-2015) and Minister of State for Defence in the 2010 Coalition. Nick was spokesman for the House of Commons Commission, which runs and regulates the institution. He was one of four Lib Dems in the Cook-Maclennan talks before the 1997 election, which agreed with Labour a programme of constitutional reforms for the following Parliament, when was a Lib Dem spokesman on constitutional reform. A former CEO of the Lib Dems, he has over the last decade advised the Parliaments of Egypt, Jordan, Bahrain, Kuwait and Georgia on – among other things – holding the executive to account. In July 2023, he became chief executive of the European Movement UK.

Paul Tyler

Served in Parliament as MP for North Cornwall (1992-2005) and Bodmin in 1974, and as Lord Tyler of Linkinhorne (2005-2021). Paul has been Lib Dem constitutional reform spokesman in both the Commons (2001-05) and Lords (2005- 2021), and is a former chief whip in the Commons. He has led a number of cross-party projects and publications grant-aided by the Joseph Rowntree Reform Trust (JRRT), including Reforming the House of Lords (with Ken Clarke, Robin Cook, Tony Wright & George Young, 2005), Lords Reform: A Guide for MPs (2012, before Lords Reform Bill was passed at second reading in the Commons), Funding Democracy (2013), and a Draft EU Referendum Bill (2019).

CAN
PARLIAMENT
TAKE BACK
CONTROL?

Britain's elective dictatorship
in the Johnson aftermath

Nick Harvey
Paul Tyler

THE REAL PRESS
www.therealpress.co.uk

Published in 2023 by the Real Press, together with Radix
Big Tent and the Democracy Network.
www.therealpress.co.uk
© Nick Harvey and Paul Tyler.

ISBN (print)   978-1912119349
ISBN (ebooks)   978-1912119332

Dedicated to Kate & Nicky (& all long-suffering political partners).

Acknowledgements

We are very grateful to all who have so generously given encouragement, advice and factual correction. They are too numerous to list without inadvertently causing offence. In any case, we are entirely responsible for all opinions and any errors!

Nick and Paul

Contents

1

Foreword

Hannah White

Director, Institute for Government

Democratic reforms in the later twentieth and early twenty-first century – on standards in public life, effective scrutiny and topicality of the parliamentary agenda - rebalanced power away from the executive and towards Parliament. But the last decade of political instability and constitutional flux has undermined that progress, shifting power back towards the executive and raising urgent questions about the strength of our parliamentary democracy.

The anticipated 2024 general election presents a critical opportunity to reflect on the problems which have been revealed or exacerbated by the successive disruptions of Brexit, Covid-19 and the cost of living crisis. This timely and readable volume – produced by two experienced former parliamentarians, with extensive knowledge of parliamentary systems at home and abroad – is an important intervention in the debate which is now so urgently needed.

The authors offer a sweeping menu of improvements which could be made to our parliamentary democracy, while prudently flagging the reality that any government in power will be tempted to cling on to its existing levers rather than empower Parliament in the ways they propose. As they acknowledge, no reader is likely to agree with every reform they propose, but their expansive menu usefully highlights the numerous ways in which our political system might be reformed.

This book should offer much food for thought for all those in a position to remedy the deficits in our democracy both now and in the future.

Foreword 2
Lord Lisvane
Former clerk of the
House of Commons

Most people are unaware of that web of statute, Parliamentary standing orders, precedent (and occasionally plain common sense) which is in effect the constitution of the United Kingdom. If they think about it, perhaps they are comforted by that essentially British concept, "fair play".

But we do notice the constitution when things go wrong. And over the last six or seven years, things have gone very wrong. Of course, one cannot discount political reality. governments want to win; secretaries of state want to push "their" legislation forward; the elected House hears the drumbeat, however faint to start with, of a forthcoming general election. And politics may be about people; but our institutions should be strong enough to withstand the occasional bad apple or selfish venality.

Alas, recent events have brought us to the point where few constitutional certainties can be relied upon; and where power has leached away from Parliament to an over-mighty executive which is no longer held to effective account.

In the opening paragraphs of this excellent work, the authors present a merciless charge sheet of what has actually gone wrong over the last decade. The reasons are various: carelessness, poor judgement, ignorance, sectional feuding, abrogation of responsibility – even in some cases malevolence.

Paul Tyler and Nick Harvey are assiduous and determined advocates of constitutional reform; and they are armed with many years of practical experience. They acknowledge that not everyone will agree with all their proposals – it would be strange if it were so.

But what they put forward is shrewd and timely. It offers a much-needed constitutional cure. And it will be ignored at peril.

Introduction

British democracy has been through an extended nervous breakdown in recent years and has yet to emerge the other side, though it is to be hoped that a general election expected in 2024 might prove to be the trigger for a gradual process of recovery.

The global financial crisis of 2008 undermined the credibility of our financial institutions, just as the expenses scandal was damaging Parliament. The election which followed, in 2010, resulted in a hung Parliament and started an extended period of austerity - with calamitous consequences in widening both social inequality and political division.

This in turn led to the disastrous and wholly avoidable Brexit referendum of 2016, Labour's catastrophic experiment with Corbynism, Theresa May attempting to initiate the Brexit process without reference to Parliament and her subsequent imprisonment by her party's anti-European, nationalistic, right wing. Her ill-fated attempt to escape their clutches through another election in 2017 resulted in another hung Parliament.

As if all that weren't bad enough, Boris Johnson's opportunist seizure of power – his outrageous Trump-like attempt to prorogue Parliament, his 2019 election victory on a fraudulent manifesto, and the predictable denouement of his downfall in disgrace – was followed by the brief nightmare of Liz Truss and Kwasi Kwarteng, and now Rishi Sunak - a level-headed man out of his depth and in a hopelessly weak position attempting forlornly to defy political gravity.

Our purpose

The destructive legacy of the Johnson years warrants comprehensive analysis and radical remedy. One damaging feature of that legacy is the further gross deterioration in an already unhealthy relationship between Parliament and government. This is a pivotal intersection of power within the UK constitution, but the legacy will become permanent unless strong remedial action is taken urgently.

How should an incoming government address this quagmire? Our purpose here is to explore this one particular aspect of the constitutional rehabilitation which is now both sorely needed and increasingly viable. With a change of government looking ever more likely, attention is turning to political renewal.

Sir Keir Starmer turned a very welcome focus onto constitutional reform in December 2022, in publishing A New Britain: Renewing our Democracy and Rebuilding Our Economy, produced by a commission chaired by former Prime Minister Gordon Brown. Starmer has vowed to undertake a root-and-branch reform of the UK constitution, saying that politics is 'broken'. Even so, the prospectus offered so far has (hugely welcome) ideas for Lords reform and devolution of power from the centre to localities, but not a great deal more.

This presents the risk that, once those two subjects were addressed in power, a tickbox mentality might lead Labour to conclude that constitutional reform was 'done'. In that case, the opportunity to shake up our political culture from top to bottom – which Starmer appears to recognise is needed – will be missed.

That would be a tragedy. With Labour's conference having also voted for electoral reform, the climate is better than at any point in almost thirty years for promoting radical change.

One lesson Liberal Democrats learned from the ill-fated coalition with the Conservatives was the danger of pursuing change via a 'business as usual' modus operandi. Allowing the Tories to operate as if running a single party government made it much more difficult to impact upon outcomes. Similarly, radical political change after a 2024 election risks being undermined both in practice and principle if the pivotal relationship between the executive and legislature remains in the state into which it has now descended.

Put simply, in a proudly proclaimed 'parliamentary democracy', the executive is accountable to the legislature, and not the other way round. Lord Hailsham, in his 1976 lecture, warned of the perils of 'elective dictatorship' but things have only got worse since then.

This under-explored aspect of political reform receives too little comment or study and needs steering onto the agenda now, to make it part of any post-election renewal. Our aim is to promote such discussion.

We examine our subject in sequence: starting with the corrupting effect of flawed election legislation which denies a level playing field; moving on to media hysteria causing undue haste in appointing new governments; the need for a sovereign Parliament to set its own agenda and timetable; and powers for strong committees with real teeth to force changes on government through Parliamentary resolutions.

We then consider how governments can abuse power: the racket of 'government by diktat' which would have made even Henry VIII blush; the Royal Prerogative – ancient powers which invite Prime Ministerial megalomania; the tattered remains of the Ministerial Code; ideological witch-hunts against top civil servants not deemed to be 'fellow-travellers'; the 112-year wait for a democratic second chamber; and our descent to the point where politics is on sale to the highest bidder, whoever they may be.

It is hard to estimate the public appetite for a stronger Parliament. They elect Parliament – they do not elect the government. But they did not much like it when Parliament cut up rough with government about Brexit, so perhaps they are psychologically ingrained with the idea that strong government must always get its way. By contrast, American and French electors often knowingly vote for 'cohabitation' with its creative tensions between legislature and executive.

We hope there may be interest across parties and beyond. The enthusiasm with which the present Lord Hailsham has encouraged us to add his father's Elective Dictatorship lecture as an appendix to this book may be indicative.

Lord Hailsham's 'elective dictatorship'

The dangers inherent in Lord Hailsham's 'elective dictatorship' have been all too evident in recent years – on a scale likely to have this true Tory spinning in his grave (he died in 2001). Yet there is a distinct danger that the specific issue of the practical relationship between executive (Government) and legislature (Parliament) will be overlooked in the encouraging discourse now emerging around political reform, and that the next Parliament will simply default to business as usual. This vital piece of the jigsaw needs careful stewarding into place.

In opposition, Labour presents a keen reform narrative because it is the outsider offering change to an outdated, anachronistic and even corrupt political system. In office, however, they would become the insider – with a risk of their soon concluding (as the Blair administration did) that there are distinct advantages to largely untrammelled executive power.

Keir Starmer's bold promise to 'clean up Westminster' will only be partially fulfilled if it focuses narrowly on behavioural standards - important though they are - and fails to grasp the point that Westminster must fundamentally reform its own power balance and culture as well as driving further welcome devolution.

Stimulating debate

The authors are well-versed in the shortcomings of existing processes, having both spent parliamentary careers largely in opposition, but frequently working across party lines on reform issues. That is not to suggest that we are uniquely sighted on this, but we are concerned that nobody else in politics seems to be pushing this specific agenda right now – though many will doubtless sympathise with it.

Our proposals here constitute a 'maximalist' agenda. No reader is likely to agree with each and every suggestion we make. Following publication of the book we plan to circulate it to relevant people and organisations, engage in debate and participate in events.

We aim to build bridges with others to promote this urgent agenda before the window of opportunity for action is missed.

List of proposals

1. Election law

- Consolidate the Representation of the People Act (RPA) 1983 and Political Parties, Elections and Referendums Act (PPERA) 2000 into one election law Act, simplified and updated.
- Give the Electoral Commission total independence, with sole power to draft election regulations.
- All campaigning resources deployed in a seat to count towards the spending limit in that seat (including advertising, direct mail, social media, phone-calling, push-polling, VIP visits, and future innovations).
- Set seat spending limits realistically high, but not so high as to turn elections in a pastime for the rich.
- A corresponding major reduction in parties' national election expenditure limits.
- Relax or widen the voter ID requirements at polling stations to ensure maximum participation.

2. Changes in government

- A Commons vote to approve the appointment of a Prime Minister, cabinet and government.
- Parliament to set its own post-election timetable for convening, appointing its Speaker and select committees, and promulgating its own standing orders.
- Select committees to conduct confirmatory hearings for cabinet posts, and only after all these preliminary steps, to vote to appoint a government and consider a King's Speech.
- At the start of a Parliament, a set period for all such

preliminaries – perhaps a month or six weeks.

● The constitutional norm to be the incumbent PM and government staying on as caretaker until the new one is appointed.

3. Allocating parliamentary time

● Commons agenda set by a business committee comprising government, opposition and back-benchers.

● The chair, who should not be a minister, to be an MP elected by back-benchers for this purpose.

● Government business to be capped at a set proportion of parliamentary time (eg, 50 or 66 per cent).

● Private Members' Bills to have more time (Monday mornings?) and vote at the House's convenience.

● Non-government business to be expanded – including bills, motions, committee reports and petitions

● Parliament to set its own sitting hours, weeks, and schedule – and summon ministers accordingly.

● All e-petitions meeting a signature threshold to be debated in the House, with a minister responding.

● All resolutions of our sovereign Parliament to be binding on government.

4. Parliamentary committees

● Select committee findings, if endorsed by resolution of the Commons, to be binding on government.

● Clear statutory powers to summon ministers, officials, citizens and visitors to appear before them.

● Criminal offence of Contempt of Parliament with fines and ultimately detention in the Tower of London.

● Permanent 'legislative scrutiny committees' for each department – or groups of departments.

- Such committees to handle secondary legislation, deciding to what extent to examine, amend or block.
- Regular pre- and post-legislative scrutiny by these new or select committees, or a mix, and Lords.
- Chairs and members of select and legislative committees to be directly elected by secret ballot of MPs.
- Adequate staffing and resources for committees to scrutinise departments and legislation thoroughly.

5. Scrutiny of secondary legislation and regulations
- Parliamentary procedures should prohibit Henry VIII clauses and making law by 'public notice'.
- Clear distinction between informal wishes of government in guidance, and the requirements of the law.
- Reaffirm the Ponsonby Rule, enabling Parliament to supervise all significant UK international obligations.
- Reiterate the right and responsibility of each House to reject any inadequate Statutory Instrument.
- All delegated legislation should be amendable with wider options than simple 'all or nothing' rejection.

6. The Royal Prerogative
- Rationalise and codify prerogative powers, their limitations and processes, fit for the 21st century.
- Establish a general and binding principle that any PM wishing to use prerogative powers must first secure a two-thirds majority in a Commons vote – including for any early dissolution or prorogation.
- Government to secure parliamentary approval when committing the Armed Services to significant military deployment, beforehand where practicable and swiftly thereafter where not.

• Repeal the section of the Dissolution and Calling of Parliament Act 2022 which prevents anyone seeking judicial review of ministers' interpretation of this legislation.
• Review the case for wider repeal of that Act; and remove the absurd anomaly of one political team leader (the PM) being effectively equipped with a 'whistle to end the match at a time of their choosing' (to pick the date for a general election).

7. The Ministerial Code
• Give statutory underpinning to the Ministerial Code, enshrining the Seven Principles of Public Life.
• A Commissioner for Ministerial Standards, with complete independence and powers to investigate.
• State penalties applicable to ministers, with the assumption that breach of the Code means they depart.
• Enact all recommendations of the Institute for Government report updating the Ministerial Code.

8. Impartiality of the civil service
• Commission a review of the practical working of the Constitutional Reform & Governance Act 2010 and involve all levels of the civil service and their representatives in such exercise.
• Only the Cabinet Secretary to have powers to remove a Permanent Secretary from a department – and only on performance or disciplinary grounds, which can be tested in law.
• Clarify that the role of special advisors (spads) is to advise ministers, with no power to instruct or direct civil servants.

9. Reform of the second chamber

● Build on the widely-backed 2012 House of Lords Reform Bill as the starting template for change.

● Adopt its largely or wholly elected second chamber of around 450 members, directly elected by STV in multi-member regional (English) and national (Scotland, Wales and Northern Ireland) constituencies.

● Elect third of the members every 4-5 years, so that MPs always have a more powerful recent mandate.

● Non-renewable 12 or 15-year terms would give a longer outlook, with more independence from parties.

10. Standards in public life

● Enact the recommendations of the Committee on Standards in Public Life (CSPL)'s 2021 report *Upholding Standards in Public Life* with strong independent regulators.

● Enact the principles of the CSPL's 2011 report *Political Party Finance*, with limits on donations, reduced expenditure limits and a modest increase in the existing level of state funding.

Chapter 1
Flawed election laws
Our corrupt legislation is denying a level playing field.

- Consolidate the RPA 1983 and PPERA 2000 into one election law Act, simplified and updated.
- Give the Electoral Commission total independence with sole power to make election regulations.
- All campaigning resources deployed in a seat to count towards the spending limit in that seat (including advertising, direct mail, social media, phone-calling, push-polling, VIP visits, and all future innovations).
- Set seat spending limits realistically high, but not so high as to make elections a pastime for the rich.
- A corresponding major reduction in parties' national election expenditure limits.
- Relax the voter ID requirements at polling stations to ensure maximum participation.

The integrity of each and every constituency election campaign is the foundation of our parliamentary democracy. But Britain in 2023 is a long way from this, and flawed legislation is making a bad situation worse. Rigorous reporting and effective limiting of campaign expenditure in constituencies must be restored as a matter of urgency.

In an early attempt to frighten backbench MPs into grudgingly backing off from their intention to topple Boris Johnson, his close ally Jacob Rees-Mogg told BBC2 *Newsnight* that, "*a change of leader requires a general election.*" He claimed that, effectively, we now have a 'presidential system' and that "*the mandate is personal rather than entirely party.*"

It was pointed out that this was nonsense by Peter Riddell (former Commissioner for Public Appointments and director of the Institute for Government), by former Conservative cabinet minister Rory Stewart, by William Wragg (Conservative chair of the Commons Public Administration & Constitutional Affairs Select Committee) and by many others. We do still have a parliamentary democracy, with the Prime Minister answerable to MPs, not the other way round.

As a previous Leader of the House of Commons, Rees-Mogg should have known better. His interpretation of the function of MPs and of the constitution of a parliamentary democracy was both nonsensical and revolutionary. He was just playing juvenile politics in the hope of brow-beating colleagues with slim majorities, against a background of woeful opinion polls.

For a rogue Prime Minister faced with the collapse of his government, yet knowing alternative leaders could command a Commons majority, to seek a dissolution from the monarch on this basis would be to put the latter in a totally impossible position.

This was floated again in the dying days of the Johnson Junta in July 2022. His devoted disciples and No. 10 spinners kept repeating the claim that he personally had a massive 'mandate', just as his ministerial and Commons colleagues were deserting him. His pitiful exit speech implied the same, echoing some of the Trump delusions, to the dismay of many colleagues and commentators.

Playing partisan games with constitutional principle

The circumstances of his ejection, the machinations of the Liz Truss election (by just 80,000 Conservative party members) and the final fratricidal outcome, all added to the sense of constitutional chaos and confusion. Even Rees-Mogg struggled to explain how his theory of a national presidential plebiscite giving a credible mandate to British Prime Ministers could ever be sustained.

In the mêlée that followed the resignation of Truss, the public understandably wanted a general election, not an elite private selection of another Conservative leader and Prime Minister. With many self-appointed pundits arguing that the UK now has a presidential constitution (which suited their preferred outcome), it was scarcely surprising that 78 per cent of the electorate favoured a national vote.

Rishi Sunak attempted to square the circle by emphasising the Tories' collective commitment to the 2019 manifesto, claiming as a consequence a continuing mandate. In the fraught and frantic events of October and November 2022, with so many discarded policy intentions, that did not sound very convincing. Such a clash of party power and public impotence is inherently unstable in a representative democracy.

Even taking into account the peculiar circumstances of the 2019 election – when Jeremy Corbyn could have been just as much a factor as Johnson himself in securing the Conservative majority – our parliamentary system denies a party leader a personal mandate, which comes only if he or she commands a Commons majority. Johnson and Rees-Mogg may not like that, but they and their colleagues should at least know that MPs win seats, and then together build government majorities. Hence the crucial significance of the integrity of those constituency contests and results.

Battleground seats

For decades, UK general elections have seen some 500 constituencies where the campaign has been of little significance, and another 150 which determine the entire outcome. The targeting of funds and other resources (like professional staff) into key battleground seats, in preparation for and during those final weeks, has been crucial in securing a Commons majority. All major parties have exploited a gaping hole in election law to inflate their national investment in these marginal or target seats.

The sums involved have completely dwarfed the modest allowable expenditure for which local candidates and their agents must report and are legally accountable – less than £20,000 – making a total mockery of constituency spending limits. Just in those last few weeks before polling day, a well-endowed national party can deploy millions of pounds in a concentrated effort to win these seats, with almost no constraints and minimal transparency.

This escalation of external influence has been greatly enhanced by developing campaign methods. With fewer active members to rely on to make contact with residents, the arrival of sophisticated electronic communication, precise mailshots and call centre operations have become favoured investments.

An individual voter, in a marginal seat, can be targeted with a tailored message to encourage support for a specific candidate without any local involvement. The link between the candidate's campaign and this hugely expensive activity on his/her behalf is broken, and neither the relevant local returning officer nor the national regulator – the Electoral Commission – can piece together an audit trail of the whole picture.

Inadequate controls

Already the Commission has been thwarted in attempts to tighten up controls. The 2018 Supreme Court Judgement (R v Mackinlay and others 2018 – UKSC 42) sought to clarify the Representation of the People Act 1983 (RPA) by demonstrating continuing local responsibilities.

The national Conservative Party had invested large sums and deployed professional staff to head off a UKIP threat in the South Thanet constituency. The judgement wisely ruled that such expenditure must be declared as election expenses by the candidate, *"even if the items provided have not been authorised by the candidate, the candidate's agent or someone authorised by either or both of them."*

The Commission recognised the need for better guidance. It published draft codes of practice in 2018–20, which rightly attempted to define all activities for which the local campaign (candidate and election agent) should be held accountable. The Tory government chose not to submit these to Parliament for approval.

Nefarious legislation

Instead, in pretence that 'clarification' of the judgement was required, ministers set about relaxing the rules significantly. In their Elections Act 2022 they introduced a clause to specify that:

"Property, goods, services or facilities are made use of on behalf of a candidate only if their use on behalf of the

candidate is directed, authorised or encouraged by the candidate or the candidate's election agent."

This definition seems highly elastic, with the Commission concerned that it could expand to enable a party's national campaign – for which ministers are pushing an increase of the limit by around £10 million from the 2019 figure of £19.5 million – to pour in cash to win those target seats, without much effective monitoring.... so long as the local candidate and agent claim ignorance.

Their only possible rationale for the huge increase must be that they plan even greater investment next time, with relaxed controls and less transparency, in 100 or more target constituencies. This insidious change went largely unnoticed amidst the public outcry at the Act disfranchising any elector arriving without allowable photo ID (negating a fundamental principle of the RPA).

Ministers also snuck in a new clause replacing the partly preferential voting system for mayoral and police commissioner elections with First-Past-The-Post (FPTP). This had not been the subject of any consultation and the system originally chosen, with all party support, has been widely recognised as ensuring that the winning candidate enjoys support of a majority of those voting. However, it seems the 'supplementary vote' system did not adequately distort votes in favour of Conservative candidates. Indeed, this retrograde change, in May 2023, resulted in their success in Bedford, on a risible minority of the vote – less than a third.

Armed with this fresh distortion, the Sunak government threatens to impose elected mayors on more top tier local authorities, even those which want to retain broader cabinet leadership. Coupled with FPTP, this would concentrate yet more power in individuals with minority mandates: local 'elective dictators'.

Attempt to hobble the Electoral Commission
The Act also threatens new constraints on the operations of the Electoral Commission, which can be imposed by the Speaker's Committee – which has an inbuilt majority of MPs from the governing party. Commenting on that, the chair of the Commission, John Pullinger, was scathing: *"Powers... like that are inconsistent with the Electoral Commission acting as an independent regulator."*

As a meticulously non-partisan public servant, Pullinger also declared witheringly that *"most people would think that the government of the day has only one strategy and policy priority for the next election, and that's to win it for themselves."* The Commission was set up with explicit cross-party endorsement after the sleaze crisis of the 1990s, and all its members (except the Conservative nominee) expressed concern at the Act's provisions. It should be getting more powers, not fewer.

A determined effort in the Lords to mitigate this threat, led by the convenor of the crossbenchers, Lord Judge, failed in the final parliamentary 'ping-pong' votes at the end of the 2021/22 Session, when 100 Labour members out of 167 absented themselves for whatever reason, and the vote was lost.

However, the implicit government threat to impose a new 'directive statement' on the Commission (it has even drafted one) remains controversial. So much so that even the Speaker's Committee itself has expressed serious concern. In its report published on 22 December 2022 it concluded, *"the [ministerial] draft statement is currently neither necessary, nor likely to assist the Commission in its pursuit of the aims and objectives already approved by the Speaker's Committee and adopted by the Commission."*

It would seem that the whole invention is intended as a veiled threat to keep the Commission from being too independent and impartial. Bear in mind that no fewer than three government ministers serve on the Speaker's Committee, which has a majority of Conservative members. Perhaps they were anticipating a future government taking a different view of clashing claims of electoral advantage?

Seats being bought

Beside these other more emotive issues, the impact on target seats and therefore on likely Commons arithmetic, seems to have been overlooked. The level of outside party expenditure has rendered the limits on constituency spending impotent. Seats can now be 'bought' in the manner of the old 'rotten boroughs', which successive legislation since 1883 has sought to outlaw.

Parallel plans to relax rules on the use of personal data will trigger burgeoning investment in direct mail, phone banking and other communication, further distorting local campaigns. Enlisting and deploying millions of pounds – rather than seeking millions of new supporters – seems to have been the objective of the Johnson government.

As part of the relaxation of controls, the Conservatives were desperate to enable more overseas residents to make political donations. By extending overseas electoral registration eligibility to life, rather than for just 15 years after leaving the UK, they calculated that their central party coffers could hugely benefit. A few more votes were of less interest to them than millions of pounds.

There is another surreptitious side-effect. If the incumbent MP in a potentially marginal seat is dependent on central party funding for his or her continuing parliamentary career, then pressure from the hierarchy or whips becomes even more pervasive. Few now have other careers to fall back on. A threat to remove huge sums of support could bring a member into line even quicker than traditional forms of intimidation. The allegations about Gavin Williamson's persuasive methods as chief whip should leave no one underestimating the impact on individual MPs.

Urgent need to overhaul electoral law

Both the Law Commission and Committee on Standards in Public Life (CSPL) have consistently proposed that the two parallel sources of electoral law – the RPA 1983 and Political Parties Elections & Referendums Act 2000 (PPERA) – should be brought together, simplified and updated. This is now urgent.

They have also stressed that such a new foundation for UK representative democracy would need the fullest consultation, clarity and consensus.

The critical change needed is that all campaigning resources deployed in a seat should count towards the spending limit in that seat – including advertising, direct mail, social media, phone-calling, push-polling, VIP visits, and whatever other wheezes campaigners dream up in the future. The seat limit needs to be set at a realistically high level to cover this, but not so high as to make the whole thing a pastime for the rich.

Such was the Contempt the government had for the

CSPL – an independent watchdog – that they ignored all its recommendations to tighten up lax rules for campaign donations and expenditure. The CSPL had consulted and examined complaints in detail, but ministers instead chose to pursue Conservative party partisan advantage and the changes made by the Johnson government led in totally the wrong direction.

The lack of transparency and accountability is also very relevant to referendums. Most participants in elections are identifiable and accountable after polling day. Even so, some shadowy protagonists in referendum campaigns disappear as fast as they have appeared, without anyone really knowing where on the globe they or their finances came from. In the final days of the 2016 EU Referendum vast sums were spent by temporarily contrived 'front' organisations – for example on social media activity – but by the time their intervention had been noted, some had become untraceable.

Botched constituency boundaries

One change in political geography may prove less controversial than anticipated. Constituency boundary changes in the summer of 2023 were expected to distort party prospects, or remove existing distortions – according to one's point of view. Conservatives have long argued that the varying size of constituency electorates gives a big advantage to Labour, although in truth, differential turnouts between seats exaggerated the effect. This 'removal of discrepancies' was originally expected to give the Conservatives 15 or so more MPs.

During the passage of the legislation which sought to equalise the numbers of voters in each constituency, the

Conservatives succeeded in maintaining a very tight 5 per cent variance from the 'mean' target number. Opposition parties sought to relax this to 10 per cent, to take account of well-established historic communities.

The Conservatives may live to regret their over-strict limits. With the different circumstances now in many of the 'Red Wall' seats in the North and Midlands, experts estimate that the changes will produce minimal advantage for the party. There will be a reduction in Welsh Labour MPs, but the overall benefit to the Conservatives could be as few as six seats, with some messy 'blue-on-blue' contests for new seats perceived as winnable. The net result are contorted constituencies which don't even provide the intended maximum Conservative advantage.

Constitutional contortions

The central challenges to our constitution remain, by no means dispelled by the defenestration of Boris Johnson. We are brought back to the core relationship between Parliament and government. The overall picture is not one of ignorance, but of planned distortion and certainly not of reinvigorated democracy.

The extent to which eligible electors may be prevented or discouraged from voting by the new photo ID requirements echoes Republican efforts at 'voter suppression'. The government insisted on limiting eligibility to all forms of ID likely to be carried by older people, from bus passes to pension details, but student railcards and rent books are excluded. The partisan bias was too obvious to be accidental.

Whether it succeeded in distorting the May 2023 local authority elections in the Conservatives' favour is still a matter of conjecture. The party's older supporters amongst some of the so called 'Red Wall' seats may have been affected by lack of passports and driving licences.

Throughout all the areas with elections, it certainly stopped some of those qualified to vote from doing so. Some councils have provided figures. In Walsall, 1,240 intending voters were turned away as having no approved photo ID, of whom 767 did not return. In Bradford, 1,261 were turned away, with 498 not returning. An unofficial estimate suggested 1.2 per cent of those planning to vote were excluded. The Electoral Commission reported more precisely that at least 14,000 intending voters had been turned away, and failed to return.

This must be an under-estimate, because those turned back by 'greeters' were not even recorded. The *Guardian* calculated 400,000 were probably denied their democratic rights. How many more were so aware of their lack of ID that they didn't even try to go to the poll?

No doubt, if the analysis does suggest that the Conservatives suffered from their own discrimination, there will be an attempt at revision before the forthcoming general election, when higher turnout could take absentee numbers nearer to a million. With Jacob Rees-Mogg's confession (15 May 2023) – despite his own role in introducing the ID requirement – that the intended 'gerrymandering' had proved counter-productive, this seems inevitable.

Increasing the ability of millionaires to sway campaigns, which are determined in battleground seats, is following America's example. The November 2022 US mid-term elections clocked $9.7 billion total campaign expenditure, up some 144 per cent since the previous elections. The

British public is fearful that our system is drifting in the same direction. It is concerning how many donors are naturalised citizens of Russian descent.

Money talks. The demand for donations will escalate, and the whole integrity of our representative democracy is being tarnished with yet further inflation of campaign cash, and pernicious relaxation of already flawed and inadequate controls. The aim is an outcome which corrupts the true public will.

Chapter 2
Changes of government

**Media hysteria causes undue haste – Parliament
must set the pace.**

- A Commons vote to approve the appointment of a Prime Minister, cabinet and government.
- Parliament to set its own post-election timetable for convening, appointing its Speaker and select committees, and promulgating its own standing orders.
- Select committees to conduct confirmatory hearings for cabinet posts, and only after all these preliminary steps, to vote to appoint a government and consider a King's Speech.
- At the start of a Parliament, a set period for all such preliminaries – perhaps a month or six weeks.
- The constitutional norm to be the incumbent PM staying as caretaker until the new one is appointed.

Few images so encapsulate the inelegant haste with which Britain changes its government than that of Ted Heath's piano being unceremoniously bundled out onto the steps of 10 Downing Street within hours of Harold Wilson agreeing to form a minority government in March 1974. (The hapless instrument had arrived with fanfare in rather sunnier circumstances after Heath took office in July 1970.)

February 1974's general election saw a narrow but clear Conservative win in votes, but an even narrower margin of just four seats in Labour's favour. Heath spent the ensuing weekend trying to persuade the Liberal leader Jeremy Thorpe to form a coalition, but neither party – nor their MPs – would wear it. On the Monday, Wilson accepted the Queen's invitation to attempt to form a minority Labour government, and it was curtains (already measured, according to cynics) for the piano.

Some 36 years later, David Cameron had greater luck in seducing Nick Clegg into a coalition, but events were again characterised by indecent haste. Although Britain was seeing the creation of its first coalition since the wartime National Government, negotiations were concluded, and the government formed, in just a few days. This speed came back to haunt the Lib Dems – indeed, it still does to this day.

International comparisons

Such haste is in marked contrast to the practices not only in countries which habitually see coalitions needing to be formed, but also with transition arrangements even in many which do not.

In the **United States**, the president-elect has roughly eleven weeks to prepare to take over administration of the federal government from the incumbent president. Congress provides funds for the transition in the period between a winner emerging from polling on the first Tuesday of November, through to inauguration day on 20 January, when the president-elect takes full power. In fairness, the difference in political system – with the president appointing some 9,000 or so governmental posts (often taking much of the first year) – means there is much to do in those weeks.

In **Germany**, where it is almost always necessary to form a coalition between parties to build a majority government, all the parties can hold 'exploratory talks' to determine if they can work together despite ideological differences. Once some parties decide a coalition seems possible, they get into detailed negotiations on policy issues, ministerial appointments and working arrangements. Only once they have signed a coalition contract of terms and agreements can they then nominate a Chancellor to be appointed by the Bundestag.

After the 2017 election, it took more than five months before Angela Merkel was formally confirmed as Chancellor. After the 2021 election, which saw the SPD gain a small advantage over the CDU, it seemed Merkel would have to continue as caretaker Chancellor for many months, potentially into 2022. In fact, three parties finalised a deal in about two months, outlined in a detailed 177-page Contract. Olaf Schulz took office and Merkel left just a few weeks shy of achieving the record for longest-serving Chancellor.

The **Netherlands** is known for long transitions and a new government was installed on 10 January 2022, almost ten months after its election, the longest such negotiations in Dutch history. The coalition consists of the same four parties in which had already been in power since 2017, but it took almost 300 days to bring them back together after the March 2021 elections produced an inconclusive result.

The lack of a fully-functioning government does not seem to have hurt the Dutch economy. It rebounded strongly from a Covid-19 slump and boasts one of the strongest growth rates in Europe, though pressing matters such as climate change, health care and the strained housing market were rather left untouched.

In 2010-11, **Belgium** set a world record of 589 days without a government but surpassed themselves in 2020 when a new Prime Minister was sworn in some 652 days after the previous government collapsed. (New elections in 2019 proved inconclusive, with the separatist right making gains in Flanders, while socialists triumphed in the Francophone region of Wallonia.)

The new Prime Minister, Flemish Liberal Alexander De Croo – Deputy Prime Minister in successive governments since 2012 – headed a seven-party coalition uniting the Francophone and Flemish Liberal, Green, and Socialist parties, and the Flemish Christian Democrats. The joke in Belgium is that politicians worry the public will come to prefer being ruled by technocratic civil servants, rather than by them!

According to the constitution of **France**, the first round of a presidential election must be held between 20 and 35 days before the transition of power when the five-year term of the current incumbent expires. As Emmanuel Macron took office on 14 May 2017, any transition of power in 2022 would have taken place on 13 May 2022. Given that the two rounds of polling are two weeks apart, it has become common for the first ballot to be the full five weeks before any handover, with the second round two weeks later – then leaving three weeks for handover preparations.

All these countries have very different political and electoral systems to each other, and to Britain. What they have in common, however, is that none subscribes to the preposterous nonsense – largely fuelled by the excitable British media – that it is a vital national imperative that, once an election is over, a new government must be formed and take the reins of power instantly. Hysteria seems to take hold in Britain, propounding notions that unless a new Prime Minister crosses the threshold of Number 10 within hours, the nation will collapse, there will be a run on the pound, a stock market wipe-out and we will all go to Hell in a handcart without even time to stop-off in Sodom or Gomorrah, nor collect £200 as we pass GO.

In reality, financial markets soon take upsets and surprises in their stride, as shown during the vastly more significant Covid and Ukraine crises. Even after the global financial crisis of 2008, many markets recovered strongly. So, a delay of a few days or weeks in forming a new government will not have the drastic consequences suggested (even the passage of months leaves European markets quite stable). Indeed, if a transition period could be normalised by writing it into our constitutional arrangements, such a delay would be 'priced in' and cause no ripple whatever.

Caretaker government

In the maelstrom which followed the 2010 election, Gordon Brown could and should have stayed on as caretaker Prime Minister (in Angela Merkel fashion) for however long it took to negotiate a coalition. Such a selfless service would have been in the national interest.

Unfortunately, a combination of political opportunism and media savagery portrayed him as being holed up in Downing Street, clinging on by his fingernails and having to be dragged out. He consequently had no choice but to leave, and the dignified manner in which he did so, hand in hand with his wife and children, was to his eternal credit.

How much more sensible it would have been if the incumbent staying on until everything was ready for a new government to take over – as is the norm in other countries mentioned – had been the default.

Instead, a coalition was formed with absurd haste. A

sketchy policy prospectus was agreed, but not in adequate detail to underpin a five-year term, with political management and machinery of government issues almost entirely ignored. The Liberal Democrats displayed breathtaking naïveté and paid a terrible price for acquiescing in keeping the civil service (which could and should have supported and advised them) out of key parts of the dialogue. By its latter stages, that government had become virtually politically dysfunctional.

It is not only, however, in the circumstances of a hung Parliament and coalition discussions, that a steadier pace in forming a new government would be beneficial. In terms of Parliament taking back control and developing a more healthy and robust oversight of government, it would always be preferable for Parliament to be more active and less docile in the early days of a new term or administration.

Appointing a government

As things stand, a government is formed and takes the reins of office without reference to Parliament. True, in a new term a King's Speech will presently have to be approved in a parliamentary vote, but that can be a fortnight later (and sometimes more). By then, ministers have got their feet firmly under Whitehall desks, have seized control of the Whitehall media machinery, executive powers and all political initiative. Government decides when to convene Parliament, proposes the standing orders for the new term and drags its feet for as long as it can over the formation of select committees – over which it has an effective stranglehold at this initial stage. It then quickly introduces some initial legislation, in which civil servants and parliamentary draftsmen have had only a short opportunity to engage.

The calendar year 2022 saw two more changes of Prime Minister part-way through a parliamentary term – as in 1976 (Wilson to Callaghan), 1990 (Thatcher to Major), 2007 (Blair to Brown), 2016 (Cameron to May) and 2019 (May to Johnson). The Tory party leadership election circus again proved an unedifying spectacle, with Parliament effectively frozen out and in limbo. That the process spanned the summer recess may have obscured this emasculation, but no formal vote is even needed to sanction the appointment of the new Prime Minister, nor any King's Speech or Budget to establish their legitimacy.

How much better it would be in all 'change of government' scenarios if Parliament asserted itself from the outset, and emulated its counterparts elsewhere in voting to appoint a Prime Minister and cabinet, and – when it coincides with a new session starting – setting its own timetable for reconvening and appointing its Speaker and select committees, promulgating its own standing orders, conducting confirmation hearings in select committees for cabinet posts, and - only after all that - considering a King's Speech and confirming a government.

Confirmation hearings for cabinet appointees

US-style select committee hearings to grill nominees to Secretary of State and cabinet posts would be an emphatic demonstration of Parliament asserting its rightful prerogative *à propos* the government, while also enabling a more robust role in holding the appointees to account thereafter. The exact formula could range from a full 'confirmation hearing' by the appropriate committee wielding an effective veto, through a formal committee recommendation (after a hearing) to the whole House prior to its voting, through to a more modest policy and programme presentation for the committee to explore and scrutinise.

Such a wholesome innovation should sensibly be obligatory whether the proposed appointment was taking place at the beginning of a new Parliament, or pursuant to a mid-term change of Prime Minister, or simply when a reshuffle produces a change of nominee. This need not be revolutionary. Since select committee membership is representative of the composition of the Commons, the natural majority should ensure it will not behave unreasonably, but would simply be doing what it is properly there to do.

At the start of a Parliament, a set period for such preliminaries – not as long as the eleven weeks in the USA, but perhaps a month or six weeks – could prevent indecent haste, give more priority to establishing the committees and set a healthier relationship between Parliament and government from the beginning.

Could this sunny upland ever become reality? Not while a majority government of any hue benefits from the existing order. A hung Parliament with a minority government, however, could be a different story.

Chapter 3

Allocating Parliament's time

**A sovereign Parliament must set its own
agenda and timetable, summoning ministers at its
convenience – not theirs.**

- Commons agenda set by a Business Committee comprising government, opposition and back-benchers.
- The chair, who should not be a minister, to be an MP elected by back-benchers for this purpose.
- Government business to be capped at a set proportion of Parliamentary time (eg, 50 or 66 per cent).
- Private Members' Bills to have more time (eg, Monday mornings) and votes at the House's convenience.
- Non-government business to be expanded – including bills, motions, committee reports and petitions.
- Parliament to set its own sitting hours, weeks, and schedule – and summon ministers - accordingly.
- All e-petitions meeting a signature threshold to be debated in the House, with a minister responding.
- All resolutions of our sovereign Parliament to be binding on government.

Nothing more surely defines and determines the relationship between a government and its national legislature than the way in which the agenda and timetable of the Parliament is determined.

Clearly, in any functioning democracy, the government must be given sufficient opportunity to present its legislative programme to Parliament, and to subject its proposals to whatever processes of scrutiny and debate are prescribed as the route by which such measures can progress to become law.

In Britain, however, the government goes far beyond that, dictating almost completely the agenda and timetable of Parliament. Government business managers determine precisely what will be debated when, and a weekly business statement is presented to the Commons by the Leader of the House (a member of the government) as a *fait accompli*.

The allocation and management of Commons time is one of the most formidable weapons in a British government's armoury. Government decides, after cursory discussion with the official opposition, how much time will be allocated to any measure – with timetable and guillotine motions tightening the noose further. They greedily hog parliamentary time (government business 'takes precedence'), allowing opposition MPs only limited opportunities to introduce topical debates ('supply days'), and certainly not to introduce legislation.

A backbench business committee is graciously permitted to pick up the crumbs from the rich man's table, in the form of topical debates on Thursday afternoons, when most MPs are heading back to their constituencies and governments sometimes can't be bothered (even if inclined) to oppose such motions, choosing instead simply to ignore the resolutions of a supposedly sovereign Parliament.

Indeed, the only substantive public bills to be introduced other than the government's own measures are Private Members' Bills, which are handled through utterly farcical procedures. Only a tiny number each year (in practice, about six) stand any chance of progressing to become law, and those must achieve a tightrope walk against all odds – to tiptoe their way through the obstacles which governments and their more bovine parliamentary supporters can lay in their path. Small wonder that foreign politicians, who can make their reputations through introducing legislation readily, observe our provisions with astonishment. Here, foolish MPs like Christopher Chope stupidly wreck their own reputations and that of parliamentary democracy by ignorantly blocking popular and uncontroversial measures like the 'up-skirting bill'.

Even for bill committees, government business managers effectively mark their own homework by decreeing the programming timetable. There is no good reason why the MPs on those committees should not at least suggest how to allocate their own time, and then (if needs be) obtain the approval of the House as a whole.

The need for reform

The lop-sided relationship between Britain's executive and legislature has long been widely observed by academics and commentators, and the prevalence of single-party governments with working majorities since 1945 has served only to embed further their dominance of Parliament.

In 1979, the development of the modern day select committees, under the creative influence of Leader of the House Norman St John-Stevas, was one of very few adjustments to shift the balance back in the other direction. Tony Blair's Labour governments, with huge majorities, introduced reforms to make conduct of government business more efficient – for example through programme and carry-over motions – but despite describing this as 'modernisation', their measures (however sensible) in reality strengthened government domination of Parliament further, rather than reforming anything meaningfully or progressively.

Towards the end of Labour's third term, with government authority waning, Parliament established a Reform of the House of Commons Committee, chaired by Dr Tony Wright MP and commonly known thereafter as the Wright Committee. It concluded that, in determining Parliament's agenda, government rarely takes account of the evident needs of the matter in hand, let alone the expressed wishes of even its own supporters, and recommended that the House should have much more scope to choose and schedule its own activities.

The Wright Committee proposed a worthwhile, but in truth quite modest, set of reforms, including:

- Chairs and members of select committees to be directly elected by secret ballot of MPs.
- Backbench business to be scheduled by the House not by ministers.
- The House should decide its sitting pattern for itself.
- E-petitions, with the potential for the public to compel an issue to be debated in the House.

Although the Labour government signalled that, if re-elected, it would not introduce these changes, the 2010 coalition put the report before Parliament and enacted two of the reforms: election of select committee chairs - though committee members remain nominated through opaque party systems managed by whips, then ratified by Commons motion - and the creation of a backbench business committee, albeit in control only of Thursday afternoon business.

A genuine Business Committee, incorporating government, opposition parties and backbench representatives, to determine <u>all</u> business of the House (common in other countries) was never even mooted, although that would seem to be the obvious way to try and balance competing interests.

Sitting hours

It is striking that the suggestion of the House determining its own sitting pattern (its hours) remains to all intents and purposes unaddressed, even though a so-called process of modernisation to (allegedly) 'family-friendly hours' took place in the Blair era. Prior to 1997, the Commons sat for 30 hours a week of public business on a set pattern of Monday to Thursday, 2.30pm to 10pm.

Since then, Tuesday and Wednesday have incrementally moved forward three hours, to 11.30am to 7pm. Thursday has moved forward five hours, to 9.30am to 5pm, which is more practical in facilitating travel back to constituencies before busy Friday activities. Mondays remain unchanged, facilitating travel back to Westminster for a 2.30pm start.

The 'hour of interruption' (close of debate) on Tuesdays and Wednesdays moving from 10pm, but only to 7pm, would hardly strike people in other walks of life as family-friendly. In practice there will then often be one or two votes, taking 15 minutes each, meaning that MPs typically cannot leave until more like 7.30pm. For those travelling to outer London boroughs, or to the wider ring of home counties seats which no longer qualify for accommodation in London, arrival home will be far too late to help put young children to bed or take older ones to evening activities. To compound this, the consequential earlier committee starts (8.55am in some cases) mean that such MPs must be up and out of home in the morning too early to be of any help with morning childcare either.

Beyond making the obvious point that the 30 hours of public business could easily be accommodated in normal working hours without impacting on MPs' weekly commuting pattern, the interesting question here is what impact this question has on the dynamic between government and Parliament. One regularly cited impediment to Parliament operating on a normal pattern is the impact this would have on government. It is said that ministers must be in their departments during the working day and that being in Parliament obstructs their business.

This is the tail wagging the dog. Parliament should run for its own effectiveness and convenience and government should fit around it – not the other way round. It is also a specious argument, which cheerfully overlooks the fact that at any point in time only one department's ministers need be in the chamber – the rest can be in their ministries. Only on days with a 'running whip' (IE votes possible at any moment) would they all need to be in Parliament, and that is already the case anyway.

The bigger point is that when Parliament feels compelled to put a minister and his or her proposals on the rack, and detain them in debate until a reasonable outcome can be secured, it is a far more effective tool to prevent the minister from either attending to their business in the day, or their social calendar in the evening, than it is simply to keep them from their bed in the night – a spectacle we have seen for decades.

Time for Private Members' Bills
Aside from the 30 hours of public business, Parliament has by custom and practice sat 16 times a year on a Friday for

five hours, to consider Private Members' Bills. Both the parsimony of this allocation and the particulars of the timetable seem to be designed to suit the government, which is traditionally hostile to many such bills.

It maximize the chances of ministers and their cronies frustrating Bills by 'talking them out', and diminishes the chances of MPs supporting the bill being able to vote for them, because to do so means delaying the end of their Westminster week - and start of constituency duties = by almost 24 hours.

If, by contrast, these sessions were scheduled for Monday mornings, while those proposing the bills would have to make an early start, other MPs would have the opportunity to participate in votes just a matter of minutes before their normal 2.30pm sitting. Deferred divisions could assist further, as would a lifting of their restriction to 16 sessions a year. This needs Parliament to assert itself, to stand up to government and set its own timetable, and deliver to ministers a *fait accompli* – rather than the other way round.

Sitting weeks

Similar frictions surround the question of sitting weeks. Our Parliament sits more weeks each year than many others, with absurd British media depiction of constituency weeks as holidays. Successive Prime Ministers have worried about the optics of a long parliamentary summer break, culminating in their insistence on idiotic September sittings prior to another break for party conferences (itself unnecessary, now the conferences largely span weekends rather than lasting a whole working week as they once did).

The shorter summer break has contributed in no small way to the maintenance crisis in the Palace of Westminster. When there was a 13-week break, contractors could come in, spend the first week setting up and the last week clearing up, and get 11 weeks of productive work done in between. Now the summer break is sometimes as little as five weeks, after the setting up and clearing up, only three weeks remain in between to do serious work.

We now face the prospect of a lengthy 'decant' – in fairness not entirely caused by the truncated summers, but surely exacerbated in its likely duration. In response, we have seen Michael Gove as a minister, saying that the House of Lords should move to either Stoke-on-Trent or Sunder land. This may have been tongue in cheek, or may betray a governmental view that the upper House is an irritant which should be exiled.

A sovereign Parliament must decide for itself

The greater point, surely, is that a sovereign Parliament should decide such questions for itself. It is most impertinent for Gove, as a minister, to be trying to throw his weight about in such matters.

Concerns about government being unaccountable during summer recesses could be addressed to a considerable extent by operating an unfettered system of Written Parliamentary Questions throughout the break, and through Oral Parliamentary Questions operating to their normal timetable, but via video-link.

In summary, if the House of Commons is to match the effectiveness of many other democratic Parliaments in holding government to account **and** crosscutting its legislation, then it simply must assert itself in setting its own agenda and timetable, summoning ministers at its convenience not theirs.

Chapter 4

Parliamentary committees

Strong committees, able to force government policy change, are vital to restoring faith in parliamentary democracy...

- Select committee findings, if endorsed by resolution of the Commons, to be binding on government.
- Clear statutory powers to summon ministers, officials, citizens and visitors to appear before them.
- Criminal offence of Contempt of Parliament with fines and ultimately detention in the Tower of London.
- Permanent legislative scrutiny committees for each department – or groups of departments.
- Those committees to handle secondary legislation, deciding to what extent to examine, amend or block
- Regular pre- and post-legislative scrutiny by these new or select committees, or a mix, and Lords
- Chairs and members of Select and Legislative Committees to be elected by secret ballot of MPs.
- Proper staffing and resources for committees to scrutinise departments and legislation thoroughly.

It is often said that the House of Commons' best work takes place in committee. This is sometimes offered as an explanation by MPs when constituents ask why TV pictures so often show the chamber very thinly attended, or why behaviour in the chamber is unruly and debate so nugatory. And in fairness much good work does take place, at least in the select committees, where party allegiance can often play second fiddle to a genuine quest for a truthful picture and constructive solutions.

None of these honeyed depictions should, however,

mask serious weaknesses in the Westminster committee system. It is absolutely essential that any Parliament aiming to hold a government to account should include in its armoury committees which are powerful, authoritative, prestigious, populated by respected MPs, and rigorous and effective in their processes. We are some considerable way short of that.

Our current select committees in the British Parliament were introduced by Norman St John-Stevas as Leader of the Commons in 1979. It was his innovation for committees to mirror government departments, paving the way for systematic scrutiny by the Commons across the whole waterfront of government activity, in his words to *"provide opportunity for closer examination of departmental policy and of the way in which ministers are discharging.... their work."*

Select committees

Select committees are generally perceived as fairly effective and successful. Further evolutionary change came in 2003 with the introduction of a modest salary for the committee chairs. (There is a myth that committee chairmanship offers an alternative political career to ministerial office, but in reality the vast majority of chairs either have been ministers, or go on to be, in rather a 'revolving door' culture.)

Then, in 2009, the review led by Tony Wright MP steered further changes, especially to the way committee chairs are chosen, removing patronage powers from party whips and instead moving to a system of election.

In the last decade or so, some committees have built a higher profile for their work, with some chairs – like

Margaret Hodge MP, while at the Public Accounts Committee – becoming powerful household names. Sometimes critics even condemn committees for grandstanding and being too hostile to witnesses.

Among those who take an interest in international comparison of legislative assemblies, however, there remains a firm consensus that the British committees lag well behind their American counterparts in power, influence and effectiveness. The real weakness compared to Washington is that they have no power to enforce their recommendations and compel changes to happen.

Select committees' strength is that they investigate issues in much more depth than is possible in parliamentary debate. Hearings occur on several different days, generally over a period of weeks, allowing a range of witnesses to be called in and questioned. This is one of the few areas where outsiders can participate directly in parliamentary proceedings.

Whilst select committees have their own staff to undertake background research, frame questions to ask, and draft reports, such staff teams are much smaller than in the US and tiny by comparison to the resources of the government they are endeavouring to scrutinise on behalf of the public

Ultimately, select committees' authority is principally limited by this lack of enforcement power. They have powers to scrutinise government departments' actions, policy, and legislation, but no corresponding power with which to force changes, leaving them somewhat 'toothless'. Government must reply to their reports (and often does so tardily and dismissively), but is not obliged to accept or act upon them – which is not a healthy power dynamic between Parliament and government, and renders at least some of their work pointless or at best marginal.

Lack of government co-operation
Sometimes committee reports have a delayed influence, where their findings may over time help tip argument inside government in favour of change. Positive media coverage of the reports helps with that.

Absurdly, although committees can technically issue a formal summons to ministers to appear before them, these are not binding and therefore the committees are reliant on goodwill. Perhaps it would be too optimistic to think that any government would introduce measures to remedy these significant systemic deficiencies – but really, in a sovereign Parliament, should such steps be within their gift?

A few committee reports are debated in Parliament - far too few! - but such debates, while welcome as an opportunity to air the report and question the minister on the government's response, are often poorly attended as debates take place on a non-substantive (adjournment) motion, so there is no opportunity to seek the House's endorsement of the report or to instruct government to take any action in response.

The value of these debates would be greatly enhanced if they were routinely debated (unless there is particular reason not to) and on a substantive motion, within a reasonable period of the publication of the report. It might sensibly be these resolutions – if passed – which should compel government to act on a report, rather than simply the committees' recommendations. (The Speaker, in consultation with the chair of the Liaison Committee, might decide whether a select committee report is sufficiently topical and significant to merit a debate on the floor of the House, or alternatively to be taken in Westminster Hall.)

Other committees — and some outside observers — complain about the substance of government responses. The Defence Committee has complained that "*departmental replies to reports are usually very defensive, often late, and show little appetite for dialogue with the committee.*" The Regulatory Policy Institute's Better Government Programme described government responses as 'models of evasion'.

In some cases, committees' work has been impeded by the department's unwillingness to provide information. The Defence Committee once reported that it had been driven by the MoD's reluctance to provide information about the history of the UK's involvement in Afghanistan to calling in retired ministers and military personnel, "*all of whom proved more helpful than their successors.*"

Committee powers less than clear-cut

The wider powers of committees to summon witnesses and papers are sometimes less clear-cut than is imagined. In 2011, the chief executive of Kraft Foods, based in the USA, refused to appear before the Business Committee to discuss the takeover of Cadbury's.

When the Culture, Media & Sport Committee summoned Rupert Murdoch and others from News International to give oral evidence on phone hacking, there was speculation that they would refuse. In the event, the witnesses complied with the summons, so the question was not put to the test. When that committee concluded that certain witnesses had misled its predecessor committee, there was general uncertainty about what could be done about it.

The behaviour of some witnesses has demonstrated Contempt for the system in the most blatant fashion. The power to put a witness on oath is not in doubt; but what would happen if a witness was thought to have lied under oath? Is the Tower of London still on standby to incarcerate such miscreants? Would a case be brought before the courts, and could this lead a court to question how the committee had gone about its business — in conflict with the ancient principle of parliamentary privilege?

In 2012, the coalition government published a consultation. Among other matters, it explored two legislative options: giving the two Houses enforceable powers by codifying their existing powers, perhaps giving the House of Commons a clear power to fine non-members; or creating criminal offences for committing Contempt of Parliament, in order to allow Parliament's powers to be enforced through the courts. Regrettably neither of these, nor any worthwhile alternative, has transpired.

Committees can enhance Parliament's reputation, and faith in democracy

Committees greatly extend the engagement of the public with Parliament in a positive way. Committees' legitimacy in the eyes of the public, their media profile and self-confidence has grown. The resources committees have at their disposal are very limited, so they need to make clever use of external support. Committees need to do more to get their message across to the public, particularly through better use of social as well as traditional media. It is desirable for their work to be respected for its integrity and relevance to people's lives, and to contribute to reviving faith in the value of parliamentary democracy.

The Liaison Committee said in 2013, "*committees should ideally be respected, listened to and feared by departments and ministers for the quality of their investigations, the rigour of their questioning, the depth of their analysis, and the value of their reports.*" Their influence should go beyond just those subjects they inquire into, with departments being mindful of the reaction of their committee when making all policy decisions, and of the high probability of exposure of any administrative shortcomings. Committees should be routinely consulted by ministers, while retaining a detachment and ability to offer objective criticism.

Select committees in the Lords are deliberately constituted to be complementary to their Commons equivalents, tasked with wide-ranging inquiries rather than mirroring departments. They suffer from some of the same weaknesses, however, with the added general impotence of an unelected House.

Bill committees need radical reform

Many Parliaments with fewer elected members (at 650, ours is one of the largest in the world) have just one set of committees to perform the two distinct roles of crosscutting both legislation and government's executive actions and policies. Indeed, the US Senate with just 100 members does exactly that. In Britain, we have sufficient numbers to operate two separate types of committees to perform the two discrete roles. Select committees scrutinise executive actions and policies; bill committees scrutinise legislation.

However, if the state of our select committees can be summarised as "good as far as it goes, but needing to go further," the situation with bill committees is altogether more discouraging and is in need of even more radical overhaul. Committees to scrutinise government legislation are formed on an ad hoc basis. So, criticism of the system often focuses on the lack of expertise among such committees, which contrasts starkly with the US culture of congressmen sometimes spending decades on a committee, developing vast expertise and stature within the sector and therefore being hugely effective at crosscutting bills.

Serving on a Westminster bill committee can be a depressing and rather sterile experience, eating up an MP's time, potentially for many weeks on end, while achieving very little because government is able to bulldoze its legislation through. This is because the numerical composition replicates the government's inbuilt parliamentary majority, which may be unavoidable but is then compounded by government whips stuffing committees with loyal back-benchers content to act as 'bed-blockers' – taking up places in order to exclude from the committee better-informed, but therefore potentially trickier, customers.

These stooges then play no real part in proceedings, but sit working on their casework correspondence (often outside in the committee corridor), remaining on hand to vote blindly when and how they are told to do so. A whip sits on each Bill Committee to ensure that the Bill goes through as the government wants. They also manage the debates, making sure that enough of their own MPs are present and influencing who speaks.

Another weakness is that the staff of such committees at Westminster largely act as passive clerks to the proceedings, like in the chamber, whereas subject-matter expertise and support in framing the questions to be probed – as in select committees – would be much more effective.

A further issue is that parliamentary scrutiny generally occurs rather late in the evolution of a bill, when government has already nailed its colours to the mast and is less amenable to amending its ideas than it might have been earlier. Pre-legislative scrutiny has been shown to be a very effective way of improving legislation by identifying potential problems earlier on and enabling solutions to be found.

Effective legislative scrutiny

Sadly, although it has been highly effective when used, particularly with joint committees of both Houses (outstanding examples are the Constitutional Reform and Governance Act 2010 and the Communications Act 2003), pre-legislative scrutiny has not become as commonplace a feature as hoped and expected.

Some critics see the solution as being to combine the work of select committees and bill committees and task one committee of MPs to fulfil both functions. The shortcoming of this idea is that we have seen in other countries' Parliaments a depressing trend for such dual-purpose committees to spend almost all their time ploughing through government legislation (and therefore responding to the government's agenda), at the expense of their own proactive investigations, probing government's executive actions and policies - and hence setting the agenda.

A better alternative, in a Parliament as huge as the UK's, is that it might well be possible to operate a system of permanent legislative scrutiny committees in parallel with the select committees crosscutting executive action. Available personnel might not stretch to one legislative committee for each department, but possibly 'themed' committees could work, covering bills from several departments in related areas (economic, social, environmental, international and so on).

There are lessons to be learned from the House of Lords as well as our former European legislation scrutiny system. Such committees should be elected openly by the House, like select committees were supposed to be, and indeed should be.

These legislative scrutiny committees might also sensibly have responsibility for secondary legislation, as in the USA, deciding when and to what extent to flag up such measures for detailed study.

This leaves the important issues of pre- and post-legislative scrutiny which could be conducted by these new committees or by select committees, or both, or a mixture of the two – sometimes involving the Lords as well. Combined scrutiny has the major advantage of anticipating later challenges – in either House – before ministers have already nailed their personal credibility to legislative detail.

In the Lords, major bills are debated very thoroughly in the main chamber, and all committee stages are examined in much more detail than in the Commons, with very little power left in the government's hands to accelerate or foreshorten business. Others are equally rigorously examined in 'Grand Committee' with any peer able to contribute. Although many amendments may be accepted by ministers, many more – however well merited – will always be overturned by the elected Commons with its inbuilt majority. The elected Commons is where the ultimate power must lie.

If Parliament is truly sovereign – and it is worth remembering that, unlike the government, Parliament is elected by the people – then it really must assert itself and become far more than simply a rubber-stamping exercise for the government of the day. This is absolutely vital to the restoration of confidence in our democracy.

An important part of this renaissance has to come through stronger and much more forceful committees. We make the point in our ' Changes of government ' chapter that American-style confirmation hearings by select committees of their department's nominated secretary of state would be a highly desirable and effective innovation. From such a bold and decisive launching point at the start of a Parliament, a transformation could take place which would make our system fit for its 21st century purpose.

Chapter 5
Scrutiny of secondary legislation and regulations

Even Henry VIII would have blushed at Johnson's 'government by diktat'.

- Parliamentary procedures should prohibit Henry VIII clauses and making law by 'public notice'.
- Clear distinction between informal wishes of government in guidance, and the requirements of the law.
- Reaffirm the Ponsonby Rule, enabling Parliament to supervise all significant UK international obligations.
- Reiterate the right and responsibility of each House to reject any inadequate Statutory Instrument.
- All delegated legislation should be amendable with wider options than simple 'all or nothing' rejection.

The Covid lockdown regulations – which the various notorious No 10 parties ignored – were never really 'laws of the land', because so many had never been scrutinised nor agreed by Parliament. They were part of the tsunami of secondary legislation issued by ministers through the long months of the pandemic.

Regulations and secondary legislation have a chequered history. On the one hand, neither MPs nor peers are equipped or inclined to check the proposed regulations with sufficient diligence. On the other hand, the mechanism for their production, evaluation and analysis has always been problematic.

The House of Commons is woefully cavalier in its

responsibility to examine these laws, which are often – and increasingly – far more significant in their impact on individual citizens, businesses and wider society than the Acts of Parliament to which they owe their origin. Party chief whips are even inclined to make nomination to the committees tasked with this role a form of penalty for backbench disloyalty.

The House of Lords is more meticulous, but the impact of its recommendations is inevitably reduced. In recent decades there have been regular attempts – largely ignored by successive governments – to overhaul the process. And yet the sheer volume and speed with which pandemic regulations poured out, following increasingly controversial use of secondary legislation for Brexit-related changes, has overwhelmed the system.

In November 2021, the two Lords select committees responsible for it, sounded the alarm. The Delegated Powers & Regulatory Reform Committee (DPRRC) published its report *Democracy Denied? The urgent need to rebalance power between Parliament and the executive,* and the Secondary Legislation Scrutiny Committee (SLSC) published *Government by Diktat: A call to return power to Parliament.*

In both cases, as the titles suggest, the committees – chaired by very distinguished Conservatives – identified a potential constitutional crisis. Significantly, neither of these two chairmen (Lord Hodgson and Lord Blencathra, formerly David Maclean MP) could be described as anti-Johnsonian.

Similar concerns were expressed in the authoritative Hansard Society Review of November 2021 and its subsequent Report of February 2023.

Henry VIII clauses

The imbalance between legislature and executive is far from new. Rather than emulating his hero, Winston Churchill, Boris Johnson seemed to follow in the footsteps of Henry VIII. His Statute of Proclamations of 1539 bypassed Parliament to give his proclamations the force of statute law. Although it was promptly repealed after the King's death in 1547, 'Henry VIII clauses' have appeared with increasing regularity in the 20th and 21st centuries.

The DPRRC reported that Henry's tactic "*now enjoys a limited revival under the veil of ministers and HMRC making law by public notice.*"

This was in the context of Brexit-related legislation. For example, the Taxation (Cross-Border Trade) Bill was full of new powers exercised by ministers through public notices. In addition, as this was a 'Supply Bill' dealing with financial issues, the Commons Speaker certified it as exempt from any scrutiny in the Lords, under long-standing rules. The DPRRC described this bill as "*a massive transfer of power from the House of Commons to ministers of the Crown*".

It is significant that those warnings predated the Covid-19 pandemic. The excuse that the emergency necessitated pre-emptive executive action overlooks the growing trend since the 2016 referendum. Covid has, however, exacerbated this threat to democratic decision-making.

Covid-19 'rules'

Justifying its tactics by claiming the pandemic demanded unprecedented urgency, the government concocted a cocktail of legislative vehicles. Despite ending up at 348 pages long, the Coronavirus Bill was not sufficient to be comprehensive, so ministers had also to rely on reference to the Civil Contingencies Act 2004 and the Public Health (Control of Disease) Act 1984.

The latter was couched in such general terms, and the powers conferred on police and magistrates so drastic, that it was bound to cause either challenge or miscarriage of justice or both. Soon enough, the police were found to be over-reacting.

Meanwhile, the lockdown had been described by the Prime Minister as an 'instruction' to the British people and the Health Secretary told MPs, *"these measures are not advice; they are rules"*. In fact, the two-metre 'social distance rule' never had the force of law, yet the police set about enforcing the 'guidance' as if it had. Boris Johnson said at his 23 March 2020 press conference – not in the Commons – that he was immediately stopping gatherings of more than two people in public and all social events except funerals. In truth, he had no such power at that stage.

The combination of a supine Commons, media frenzy and the parliamentary timetable meant that there was no serious attempt to regularise, simplify and tighten up this legislative morass even later on. For example, after these announcements on the 23 April ministers waited until the 26 April before publishing the actual lockdown regulations, by which time Parliament had adjourned on 25 March for its Easter Recess.

Throughout, ministers insisted on minimal scrutiny of their proposals, later telling the Lords Constitution Committee that the lesser degree of scrutiny for the powers under the Public Health Act was appropriate because they were not intended to authorise anything very radical. They were directed at controlling the behaviour of infected people, and were really only *"minor in scope and effect"*.

Government 'guidance'

At least there was some subsequent analysis, however delayed and desultory, by MPs and Peers. For other executive instruments, even this was lacking. A similar device to the public notice, identified by the select committees during this period, was a deliberate blurring of the distinction between delegated legislation and guidance. The former has a well-defined, if inadequate, scrutiny route through both Houses of Parliament; the latter has absolutely none.

Committees from both Houses expressed alarm. The Commons Justice Committee warned of *"potentially damaging long-term consequences, including for the rule of law."* The Joint Committee on Statutory Instruments observed in July 2021, *"there appears to have been an unwillingness to distinguish between the wishes of Government, expressed informally or in guidance, and the requirements of the law."* One does not have to be a conspiracy theorist to speculate on motives.

They were especially concerned that ministers imposed stricter controls through guidance accompanying regulations than the regulations themselves. In some cases, this guidance was used to *"amplify legislation"*, with key definitions being left for executive decision, rather than included in the regulations themselves.

Unsurprisingly, the police – let alone the public – found all this very confusing, leading to inconsistent enforcement and frequent claims of injustice. It would not be surprising if recipients of the No 10 'Partygate' fixed penalty notices resorted to claiming that their own government's inconsistent use of guidance, regulation and media briefing had led them into unwitting law-breaking!

Setting precedents

There is also a longer-term and even more concerning challenge.

Westminster is notoriously obsessed with precedents. How can we be sure that these emergency measures, justified as expedient and necessarily pragmatic, will not be used again in more ordinary circumstances?

The Contingencies Fund Bill, which MPs took just one day to dispose of in all stages after the Coronavirus Bill, authorised an additional £266 billion to be available to the government. That was an increase in the contingency provision, from 2 per cent on the previous year's annual expenditure, to 50 per cent. These measures made a mockery of the long-standing constitutional principle that Parliament's primary function is to control the way in which government spends our money.

Clearly, the detailed recommendations of the various committees will have to be implemented if these opportunistic lapses are not to become permanent. Moreover, since they reported, ministers have sought yet more devious devices to escape forensic scrutiny of controversial policy initiatives.

The Ponsonby Rule

The Home Secretary's attempt to deport asylum seekers to Rwanda was, of course, dependent on an agreement with the latter's government. However, the UK government was not enthusiastic about detailed examination by MPs or peers.

For almost a century such agreements have been subject to the 'Ponsonby Rule'. Since Arthur Ponsonby committed the Foreign Office in 1924 to enabling Parliament to supervise all agreements, commitments and undertakings involving serious international obligations, even if they were not in treaty form, no government has tried to opt out. Until now.

Faced with the expected critical examination, ministers suggested that the 2010 cross-party agreement that produced the Constitutional Reform & Governance Act (CRAG) replaced this commitment. Since CRAG didn't specifically include non-treaty agreements like that with Rwanda, they said, Parliament had no right to consider it, let alone demand to ratify its terms.

Not unnaturally MPs and peers of all parties recognised this slippery stratagem and raised the alarm. Could this too be yet another attempt at cunning precedent-setting?

Overhaul of scrutiny processes

Meanwhile, the scrutiny process in each House needs overhaul, even when the correct legislative designation is employed. Parliamentarians cannot be absolved from some blame for their own increasing impotence. A review of the conventions applying to the relationship between the two Houses of Parliament undertaken by another joint committee of MPs and peers reported in 2006. In essence, they reiterated the right and responsibility of each House to retain the ultimate sanction of a rejection of an inadequate 'Statutory Instrument' (SI).

That has only happened on a tiny fraction of occasions since World War II. Since the minister can table an identical SI next day, perhaps that is unsurprising. Otherwise, peers particularly have fallen back on voting for 'Regret Motions'. These are even more pointless. They might irritate the authors of the SI, but they have no other impact.

Inevitably members of each House tend to treat the whole process as farcical. On one occasion, peers found a devious way to avoid the false choice between impotent acquiescence and the nuclear option of outright rejection. When, in October 2015, George Osborne attempted a shortcut alternative to a full financial bill to make major changes to tax credits through a set of regulations, the Lords passed two cleverly designed motions: they *"declined to consider"* his regulations until the government had undertaken certain mitigating actions.

Ministers responded furiously, George Osborne threatening to close down the Lords. Then Lord Strathclyde, a former Conservative leader in the House, was hurriedly appointed to re-examine the issue of scrutiny of secondary legislation. Although less forthright in championing the right and responsibility of the Lords to hold government to account than he had been in opposition, even he called for reform. He wanted *"to create a procedure, set out in statute, allowing the Lords to invite the Commons to think again when a disagreement exists."*

Yet, as was speedily noted by all the relevant committees, the problem was not disagreements between the two Houses. It had nothing to do with the primacy of the elected chamber. Secondary legislation is prepared and tabled by the government. It doesn't derive from any Commons initiative and is considered simultaneously in the two Houses.

Although it might be more infrequently deployed, MPs should also have the duty to invite ministers *"to think again"*.

The DPRRC recently concluded:

"Issues relating to whether delegated legislation should be amendable and whether parliamentary procedures could be changed to provide Parliament with a greater range of options than a simple 'all or nothing' are beyond the scope of this report.... Where laws are passed with little or no scrutiny, Parliament must do more to ensure that they do not amount to an abuse of power."

Such an amending option could be a benefit for both legislature and executive, resulting in a better product for the law-abiding public.

Restoration of parliamentary control now an urgent priority

In April 2021, the Hansard Society noted:

"Since March 2020, the public has lived under some of the UK's most restrictive peacetime laws, and to support the economy public money has been spent on a vast scale. Yet parliamentary accountability for, and control over, these decisions has diminished to a degree that would have been unthinkable prior to the Covid-19 pandemic. One year on, with lockdown easing, the restoration of parliamentary control and functioning is now an urgent priority."

The Institute for Government and the Bennett Institute jointly published further analysis in December 2022, under the title *The Legislative Process: How to empower Parliament*. Their central purpose was to *"reverse the gradual erosion of Parliament's powers – accelerated by*

Brexit and the Covid pandemic – which has undermined its role and means laws can be easily passed without their impact on people and businesses being properly tested."

As strictly non-partisan and 'matter-of-fact' organisations, their recommendations should have received more attention and endorsement. For example, only about one in ten government bills receives pre-legislative scrutiny despite frequent promises from ministers, causing less effective legislation. They suggested *"a requirement on the government to publish all bills in draft form (with a waiver for urgent or emergency legislation) with a 'menu' of options for pre-legislative scrutiny,"* and giving Commons Select Committees a more pro-active role in this process.

'Laws not made in Europe without parliamentary involvement, but in Britain without parliamentary involvement'

The neutering of parliamentary scrutiny continues in 2023. Conservative Peer Lord (Daniel) Finkelstein summed it up in *The Times* on 3 January 2023 under the headline: *"Tories' dash to burn EU rules is disreputable – scrapping thousands of laws this year, as Jacob Rees-Mogg is trying to do, would be foolish and deeply anti-democratic."*

He described the minimal opportunity for examination of the consequences, and the shortcuts planned by the government, with devastating irony:

"In other words, laws will not be made in Europe without parliamentary involvement, but in Britain without parliamentary involvement. This makes a farce of the idea that we left the EU to restore democratic control over law. It is almost the definition of irony that only the unelected

Lords may now prevent the Commons from giving away its democratic powers in this fashion."

Throughout the Covid pandemic, ministers claimed that unprecedented circumstances justified these shortcuts. They also argued – even less convincingly – that they were not creating new precedents for the examination of future legislation. Yet the attempt to bulldoze through the gargantuan Retained EU Law (Revocation and Reform) Bill in just a few months in 2023 gives the lie to that.

As the bill started its process in the Lords at the beginning of February 2023, the Delegated Powers Committee issued a further warning. Led by former Conservative party chairman and Chief Whip Lord (Patrick) McLoughlin, they were scathing, calling it so lacking in substance as to be 'hyper-skeletal':

"Far from Parliament being restored to a place of primacy in relation to REUL (retained EU law), the Bill gives ministers extraordinary powers exercised by statutory instrument to dispose of, retain or rewrite REUL – including powers that involve significant and contentious policy issues. The bill contradicts pledges by the government since 2018 that Parliament would be the agent of substantive policy changes in these areas. After all, the principal constitutional argument for Brexit was that Parliament in primary legislation would make laws, rather than the institutions of the EU. Instead, the bill is full of law-making powers in relation to REUL that are given to ministers to exercise by statutory instrument."

The Sunak administration appears only too happy to continue Johnsonian tactics to evade proper parliamentary scrutiny. In May 2023, when the media – and indeed most political practitioners and commentators – were concentrating on the local elections and the coronation, an even more extraordinary example came to light.

The cross-party Secondary Legislation Scrutiny Committee in the House of Lords had been examining regulations under the Public Order Act 1986, brought into sharp relief by police action against demonstrators along the coronation route. Former Lord Chief Justice, the crossbencher Lord Thomas of Cwmgledd, a member of the committee, reported to the Lords (11 May):

"The changes to the law proposed by the Regulations were rejected by this House when they were defeated during the passage of the Public Order Act 2023 just a few months ago. As far as we can ascertain, this is the first time a government has sought to make changes to the law by making those changes through secondary legislation even though those changes had been rejected by Parliament when introduced a short while before in primary legislation. This raises a constitutional issue as to the appropriate use by government of secondary legislation, particularly as it arises in the context of an area of law which is important and attracts controversy."

When these Regulations were challenged in the Lords on 13 June, the chorus of criticism of the process adopted came from all sides. Former Lord Speaker Lady Hayman described it as "disgraceful". Former Conservative minister Viscount Hailsham referred to his father's warning of "elective dictatorship" (see the appendix). Former Commons clerk Lord Lisvane said it was "disreputable". Liberal Democrat Lord Paddick judged it a "constitutional outrage". Eminent lawyer Lord Pannick summed up the episode as *"the government seeking to obtain through the back door of Parliament what they have been denied at the front door."*

Only some wafer-thin concern not to set precedents or challenge the elected House – and abstention by Labour Peers – seems to have prevented an outright rejection vote, as advocated by Lady Jones of Moulsecoomb.

The much more damaging precedent would be if ministers – of any party – now felt they could regularly side-step effective parliamentary scrutiny, and if unelected peers felt they were neutered, unable to perform their constitutional role. That way Parliament will never regain control.

Even so, seven years after the EU referendum debate, if any administration is prepared to break with the Johnson approach and is truly concerned to enhance the 'sovereignty of Parliament', they will find a clear consensus that these issues are more urgent still and need immediate attention and radical solutions.

Chapter 6
The Royal Prerogative
**Ancient powers which just enable
Prime Ministerial megalomania.**

- Rationalise and codify prerogative powers, their limitations and processes, fit for the 21st century.
- Establish a general and binding principle that any PM wishing to use prerogative powers must first secure a two-thirds majority in a Commons vote – including for any early dissolution or prorogation.
- Government to secure parliamentary approval when committing the Armed Services to significant military deployment, beforehand where practicable and swiftly thereafter where not.
- Repeal the section of the Dissolution and Calling of Parliament Act 2022 which prevents anyone seeking judicial review of ministers' interpretation of this legislation.
- Review the case for wider repeal of that Act; and remove the absurd anomaly of one political team leader (the PM) being effectively equipped with a 'whistle to end the match at a time of their choosing' (to pick the date for a general election).

We are told that Boris Johnson's earliest recorded ambition was to be 'world king'. He may not have achieved that, but his regime was characterised by a number of attempts to enhance No 10's use of the Royal Prerogative. If he couldn't get crowned, at least he could behave regally.

The crucial problem he faced was that while this 'prerogative power' has previously remained nebulous, benefitting from the UK's unwritten constitution, as soon as codification is sought, it can become justiciable. In print, there is always more to argue over.

Over the centuries this dilemma has bemused others. As the name implies, the Royal Prerogative dates from when medieval monarchs wielded very real if not quite absolute power. Many wise words have been spoken and written as to whether, and how, the power was gradually circumscribed from Magna Carta onwards. With the Tudors and then the Stuarts, both Parliament and the courts began to flex their muscles.

After the Glorious Revolution of 1688/89, William and Mary had to accept statutory constraints in the Bill of Rights. By the 19th century, the principal residual powers were to dissolve Parliament, approve international treaties and appoint the Prime Minister. Even the power to veto a bill which had completed its parliamentary journey had died with Queen Anne. The last monarch to dissolve Parliament arbitrarily was William IV in 1834.

In the 20th century, further slippage took place, but now almost invariably towards the politicians and political parties rather than to Parliament. For example, the Crown simply accepted the advice of Conservative Party leaders in inviting one candidate – Eden in 1955, Macmillan in 1957, Home in 1963 – to form a government.

In the 21st century, all three major parties have adopted membership elections for the leadership which clarifies the choice still further, and effectively ends any royal discretion – as in 1976, 1990, 2007, 2016, 2019 and twice in 2022.

Picking a favourable election date

The power to dissolve Parliament and pick a congenial date for a general election has caused more controversy.

Whether Harold Wilson actually discussed with Palace officials the first acceptable date to seek royal consent for a new election in the summer of the 1974 hung Parliament has never been confirmed beyond doubt. Since he had no obvious obstacles for his very cautious legislative agenda the Queen could have – in theory – insisted on delay. By the autumn the case was clearer, and sure enough dissolution followed.

The curious anomaly – in a claimed parliamentary democracy – that one political team leader was effectively equipped with the whistle to end each match, in an attempt to suit his or her team's electoral prospects, was not lost on commentators.

The absurdity didn't just occur to radical reformers. Viscount Hailsham, former Conservative Lord Chancellor, drew attention to it in his 1976 Dimbleby Lecture on Elective Dictatorship:

"At the centre of the web sits the Prime Minister. There he sits with his hand on the lever of dissolution, which he is free to operate at any moment of his choice. In selecting that moment he is able, with the Chancellor of the Exchequer, to manipulate the economy so as to make it possible for things to appear for a time better than they really are. He operates the lever with his eyes fixed on the opinion polls, knowing that he is able to control in practice the loyalty of the party machine the moment the troops go into action. Criticism from below, however vocal before, is silenced until after polling day ......Thus, the dictatorship has proved more and more powerful."

Hailsham was writing this, and his 1978 book which followed, during the Wilson/Callaghan governments. The latter blew his chance of survival in 1978 by deferring the dissolution until Spring 1979, when Thatcher defeated him. The core argument of Elective Dictatorship nevertheless seems impregnable.

The Royal Prerogative in the 21ˢᵗ century

A more comprehensive series of initiatives to rationalise, codify and modernise the whole medley of prerogative powers began in the 21ˢᵗ century. The Commons Public Administration Select Committee published a set of proposals in March 2004. The Blair government failed to respond, but Gordon Brown sought to appear more sympathetic to constitutional reform, and returned to these issues as part of his 'Governance of Britain' review in July 2007.

While claiming that the "*Prerogative is a well-established part of the constitution, offering much needed flexibility to govern,*" the government also accepted that "*in many respects the prerogative is a historical anachronism.*"

The Brown government's enthusiasm for modernisation ran out of steam. Although the review listed the whole range of executive powers – ranging from treaties to recommendations to the monarch for peerages – little was agreed.

For example, in the wake of the Iraq invasion, the House of Lords Constitution Committee examined the case for a convention obliging governments to seek parliamentary approval when committing the armed services to overseas deployment. These so called 'war powers' were seen as especially significant.

As the date for the general election approached, this proposal, together with other potential codification, quietly disappeared. The eventual Constitutional Reform and Governance Act 2010 was a shrunken version of the more comprehensive array of powers examined by a joint committee of MPs and peers.

The whole Governance of Britain initiative, to which Gordon Brown had originally attached such significance, culminated with a final report which bizarrely admitted that it made *"no new proposals for reforms to the prerogative"*. Had institutional resistance in Whitehall and Westminster defeated even his government's modest objectives? The government was *"not persuaded that a statutory framework would improve the present situation."*

Fixed term Parliaments

Their successors, the Cameron-Clegg coalition, were not quite so cautious. The Fixed-term Parliaments Act 2011 was designed to achieve three necessary reforms. First, to reduce the ability of the larger partner in a coalition to pull the plug to suit their own political timetable and ditch their smaller party colleagues. Second, to give more certainty to all those – especially in business and industry at a time of great economic challenge – who hoped for some consistency, with a four- or five-year Parliament. And third, to give the House of Commons itself a role in determining if and when a shorter Parliament was justified.

By 2017, amidst the prolonged Brexit battles, this mechanism proved of limited value, although the decision-making remained formally in the Commons, rather than back in No 10.

As a result, in 2019 the incoming Johnson administration was determined to reinstate Prime-Ministerial control wherever they felt it had slipped. This began with the ill-fated executive decision to seek a Prorogation of Parliament in September 2019. The reason given by ministers – not least to the Queen – was the alleged need for time to prepare Brexit legislation without parliamentary interference or delaying tactics.

Mr Speaker Bercow (whatever his shortcomings) was a canny and consistent champion of the constitutional responsibility of the Commons. He had previously allowed a backbench initiative from Hilary Benn to seek to shut off the option of a Brexit 'No Deal', so reducing the blackmail threats from Johnson and the extreme Brexiteers. This infuriated them, and hence the attempt to shut up Parliament for several weeks.

Prorogation controversy

Even in normal circumstances, this would have been controversial. But the absence of MPs and peers would have meant that – under the Article 50 of the EU Treaty – the UK would leave the EU at the end of October automatically, with or without any agreement approved to the satisfaction of Parliament, making prorogation politically explosive.

So much for parliamentary democracy. The government's in-house lawyer, Attorney General Sir Geoffrey Cox KC MP – of richly booming voice and fortune – astonishingly told the Commons it had "*no moral right to sit.*" Fortunately, the Supreme Court thought otherwise, safeguarding the powers of Parliament.

Soon after this setback to their plans, the new government had to navigate the provisions of the Fixed-term Parliaments Act. Luckily for them, the Scottish National Party also saw party advantage in an early election (as the Liberal Democrat leader Jo Swinson also did, quite mistakenly) – which in turn forced Labour's hand. They would look weak if they opposed an appeal to the country before the final Brexit decision.

The Act's limitations on early dissolution of Parliament were therefore side-lined by a large majority vote in the Commons and the general election took place on 12 December.

Unsurprisingly, in their manifesto, the Conservatives committed to repealing the Act: easier said than done. A straight repeal would have left nothing in its place, with no statutory restitution of the Royal Prerogative. And so, the Dissolution and Calling of Parliament Bill became necessary.

Dubious legislation drafting

After scrutiny by a joint committee of MPs and peers, and by the full Commons, this bill headed into a very meticulous examination by the Lords. Led by disting-uished former judges and civil servants on the cross-benches, peers insisted on resurrecting a role for the Commons in – at least formally – deciding when the nation should be invited to elect a new Parliament. Not for the first time, our unelected Parliamentarians stood up for democracy.

Such was the casual approach of ministers that their drafting caused alarm even amongst the most loyal Conservative peers. At one point their most prominent constitutional expert – Professor Lord Norton of Louth – declared that the proposed mechanism to avoid legal challenge should be amended: *"It is constitutionally objectionable, as potentially it conflicts with the rule of*

79

law."

Others also took exception to this so-called 'ouster clause', inserted by ministers in an attempt to prevent any last-ditch resort to judicial review in the event of alleged 'misinterpretation of the legislation' by ministers. However, the amendment to remove this clause did not survive.

By contrast, the amendment relating to the role of the Commons became the subject of 'ping-pong' between the Houses in February 2022. The Conservative MPs voted obediently to deny themselves any constitutional role in deciding when they should be dissolved. The Lords, somewhat reluctantly, concluded that this self-denial – however illogical – would have to be accepted.

Does this evidence of yet another example of loss of parliamentary control render the whole situation irretrievable, or does it just amount to unfinished business? At the very least, codifying acceptable prerogative powers, their limitations and processes, in a format appropriate for the 21st century, should be a priority.

Despite this, meaningful progress will need a substantial change of attitude in Parliament – and perhaps that will only prove achievable in the event of a minority government taking office, with a majority of MPs sitting on the other side of the House and finally having a vested interest in restoring healthier checks and balances.

Chapter 7
The Ministerial Code
A 'crucial part of the spinal cord of the constitution' lies in tatters.

- Give statutory underpinning to the Ministerial Code, enshrining the Seven Principles of Public Life.
- A Commissioner for Ministerial Standards, with complete independence and powers to investigate.
- Stated penalties applicable to ministers, with the assumption that breach of the code means they depart.
- Enact all recommendations of the Institute for Government's report, Updating the Ministerial Code.

At the heart of any Parliament's effectiveness in holding a government to account lies the concept of ministerial accountability. In Britain, an important building block of that lofty principle is the Ministerial Code, setting out what can be expected of ministers and how they will conduct themselves. Indeed, the constitutional historian Professor Peter Hennessy (now a crossbench peer), describes the Ministerial Code as *"a crucial part of the spinal cord of the constitution"*.

The code is published at the start of every administration, with each new Prime Minister setting out their personal thoughts on these issues by penning, in their own words, an introductory foreword. In August 2019, just after taking office, Boris Johnson put his journalistic rhetoric to good use in his foreword:

"We must uphold the very highest standards of propriety – and this code sets out how we must do so. There must be no bullying and no harassment; no leaking;

no breach of collective responsibility. No misuse of tax-payer money and no actual or perceived conflicts of interest. The precious principles of public life enshrined in this document – integrity, objectivity, accountability, transparency, honesty and leadership in the public interest – must be honoured at all times; as must the political impartiality of our much-admired civil service. Crucially, there must be no delay – and no misuse of process or procedure by any individual minister..."

First issued to ministers in Clement Attlee's 1945 government as 'Questions of Procedure for Ministers' (though elements within it were even older), it was bizarrely kept as a government secret for several decades before being published by John Major in the 1990s. (Peter Hennessy was instrumental in bringing about this belated publication.)

As the Major government wrestled with allegations of political 'sleaze' and the Iraqi Supergun fiasco, the newly formed Committee on Standards in Public Life considered ways of updating the document, and that work came to fruition under Tony Blair as the Ministerial Code.

Heads in the sand

The Cabinet Office and civil servants issue the code to all new ministers in government, and explain its practical meaning and effect as part of the ministerial induction process. The code is wide in scope, covering ministers' conduct as part of government, within their departments, in Parliament, towards civil servants, in making appointments, their political and private interests, and travel, transport, gift and hospitality rules – all underpinned by the Seven Principles of Public Life. It is understood that breaches of the code will have consequences.

Events in recent years, notably but not exclusively the Partygate scandals, have served to highlight, however, that while medical, legal, financial and other professions have all had to accept that self-regulation has had its day, for ministers of the Crown, nothing has changed.

Even Parliament, in the aftermath of various scandals, has an independent Commissioner for Standards who can open investigations and make findings over allegations of breaches of its code, before passing them to a committee comprising MPs, alongside a strong component of independent (lay) members to determine penalties.

But ministers remain with their heads in the sand – an island of complacent self-approbation. The shortcomings of the system were exposed in November 2020, when Sir Alex Allan was forced to resign as the Prime Minister's Adviser on Ministerial Standards, after Boris Johnson rejected his finding that Home Secretary Priti Patel had bullied civil servants in breach of the Ministerial Code. The contrast with the parliamentary set-up, where the independent commissioner's findings cannot be rejected, was stark.

Sir Alex's departure, however, far from causing the political crisis it should have, in fact left a political vacuum which Johnson found rather convenient. He and his ministers adopted the Donald Trump tactics of arrogantly riding out the storm. Indeed, the *Times* political columnist Daniel Finkelstein went even further, speculating that Johnson believed the public actually liked rule-breaking (31 Jan 2023):

"*.... That they think the rules are made by the*

establishment to protect itself and not them. So politicians who are rule-breakers, are outlaws of the Dick Turpin and Butch Cassidy kind, capturing the romantic imagination as they defy the authorities. And there is clearly a demographic to whom buccaneering appeals, to whom the chaos of Johnson's personal arrangements seems like a welcome break from establishment smoothness."

He compared this to Johnson's hairstyle being consciously rather than unconsciously messy.

Serious questions about the current arrangements

It was small wonder that Lord Evans of Weardale, chair of the Committee on Standards in Public Life, observed with great British understatement that *"this episode raises serious questions about the effectiveness of the current arrangements."*

When Matt Hancock was found to have breached the code in awarding Covid-related contracts to his sister's company (in which he himself had shares!), Johnson simply declared the matter 'closed'. In the wake of this debacle, the Institute for Government published an admirable report *Updating the Ministerial Code* which rightly called for fully independent investigations and a statutory underpinning for the code.

To make an unsustainable situation worse, ministers in the Conservative government have taken steps to protect their cocooned status even further by legislating to limit the power of courts to strike down their actions as being unlawful. They have not forgotten the Supreme Court ruling about Prorogation of Parliament at the height of the Brexit melodramas. It strains belief that any reputable government in the democratic world of 2023 would attempt such Putinesque measures, and it stains the reputation of any Parliament that would permit them.

So parlous had the position become that John Major, as a former Conservative Prime Minister, was moved on 10 February 2022 to make a speech observing:

"Deliberate lies to Parliament have been fatal to political careers – and must always be so. If trust in the word of our leaders in Parliament is lost – then trust in government will be lost too.

"At No 10, the Prime Minister and officials broke lockdown laws. Brazen excuses were dreamed up. Day after day the public was asked to believe the unbelievable. Ministers were sent out to defend the indefensible – making themselves look gullible or foolish.

"Collectively, this has made the government look distinctly shifty, which has consequences that go far beyond political unpopularity. No government can function properly if its every word is treated with suspicion....

"....The lack of trust in the elected portion of our democracy cannot be brushed aside. Parliament has a duty to correct this. If it does not, and trust is lost at home, our politics is broken.

"If trust in our word is lost overseas, we may no longer be able to work effectively with friends and partners for mutual benefit – or even security."

Constitutional crisis

Peter Hennessy declared the situation under Johnson to be *"the most severe constitutional crisis,"* saying that Johnson had become *"the great debaser in modern times of decency in public and political life, and of our constitutional* conventions." He said Johnson had "*broken the law, misled Parliament and had in effect shredded the Ministerial Code,*" when he "*should be the guardian of the Code.*"

He concluded that:

"*I cannot remember a day when I have been more fearful for the well-being of the constitution. It's an assault on not just the decent state of mind which keeps our society open and clean but also on the institutions of the state. If he's not prepared to do the decent thing... why should anybody else behave decently and properly? The whole decency of our public life turns on this question.*"

Hennessy is most famed for his 'good chap theory of government': the idea that the letter of the rules is less important than the system being run by decent people who understand their spirit. This very British and pragmatic approach has always underpinned his belief that a written constitution is unnecessary. The problem now exposed is what happens when we have a 'bad chap' in charge, and this is a genie which can never be put back in the bottle.

In the midst of all this, and in the wake of the Commons voting to refer him to its Privileges Committee, Johnson breathtakingly amended the Ministerial Code, removing the requirement for ministers to resign if found to have breached the Code – they could now apologise or temporarily lose their pay instead. Staggeringly, he also removed from his own foreword all reference to honesty, integrity, transparency and accountability.

By 15 June 2022, Johnson lost another Independent Adviser on Ministers' Interests as Lord Christopher Geidt was driven to follow in Sir Alex Allan's steps, shortly after saying it was "*reasonable to conclude*" that Johnson had breached his own Ministerial Code over Covid-19 lockdown parties.

Discretion being the better part of valour, Lord Geidt did not hang around to see what response this triggered from the then-PM, who clung on to office for another three weeks before the resignation of 57 of his ministers finally forced his bitter and graceless resignation on 7 July.

Sunak omens not good

With Johnson, by grace of God, departed from No 10 – though he continued for many months to fantasise about a comeback each time his successor hit problems – his initial replacement, the ill-starred Liz Truss, mercifully lasted just 49 days. The arrival of the more sober and level-headed Rishi Sunak was expected to steady the ship, but the omens have really not been good. Despite standing on the steps of No 10 when he was appointed and declaring, *"This government will have integrity, professionalism and accountability at every level. Trust is earned. And I will earn yours,"* he has not set about doing so.

Actions speak louder than words, and he has not restored in his foreword to the code the previous references to honesty, integrity, transparency and accountability, nor reversed Johnson's watering down of penalties applicable to ministers found to have breached the code.

Furthermore, he showed worrying and very questionable judgement in reappointing to government tarnished figures like Dominic Raab with bullying accusations hanging over him, Suella Braverman just days after she admitted leaking government documents and the irredeemable Gavin Williamson. He then compounded this by trying to defend Williamson against fresh allegations about his vile conduct, before parting company with him after just two weeks in post.

After lengthy hesitation, he eventually appointed a new Independent Adviser – old Etonian investment banker Sir Laurie Magnus. But Sunak was widely criticised for refusing to meaningfully beef up the role of Magnus, who will remain unable to launch probes without first securing consent from the Prime Minister himself. Johnson's last Adviser, Lord Geidt had expressed frustration that he was unable to launch his own investigations into ministers and could only do so at the Prime Minister's behest.

Sunak said he believed he had found a candidate with the "*ability to command the trust of ministers,*" but seemed wholly insouciant as to whether his appointee would command the trust of anyone else. Angela Rayner, Labour's deputy leader, said Sunak had created another toothless watchdog... "*the rotten ethics regime he inherited from his predecessors that saw the previous two ethics watchdogs walk out.*"

The FDA civil servants' union said the Prime Minister had missed a real opportunity to "*reset the relationship*" between ministers and civil servants.

It will fall, sooner or later, to Parliament – either in the wake of yet more scandal or by taking an initiative – to get this alarming situation under control. In time, that surely means legislating to put the code onto a statutory footing and taking the other measures listed in the IfG's *Updating the Ministerial Code* report.

Privileges committee inquiry

In the meantime Parliament, having resolved that Boris

Johnson 'appeared to have misled' them in answer to MPs' frequent questions about Partygate, referred his conduct to its Privileges Committee, with its considerable powers to delve deeper. After many months of investigation, including a televised session of forensic questioning of Johnson himself, that committee produced a comprehensive 106-page report.

Johnson's dwindling band of cronies fulminated that it couldn't be proved that he had lied to the Commons. Yet the report still produced the testimonies of officials who warned him specifically that he could not say in Parliament that Covid guidelines had been followed at all times, and advised him that such assurances would not be true. That he went ahead and gave just such assurances was therefore conclusive proof that he knowingly misled the Commons.

Johnson's appalling behaviour towards the committee and its inquiry was itself a Contempt of Parliament and contributed richly to their recommendation of a 90-day ban from the Commons – way exceeding the 10-day threshold to open the risk of his being unseated. Johnson at least had the wit finally to see the writing on the wall, and quit the Commons before putting his colleagues in an even more invidious position.

Parliament was spared a tussle the likes of which had not been seen since King Charles I was summoned to Westminster Hall in 1649 and executed. But the charge against Johnson was profoundly serious, and the facts clearly proven. It is right that his Parliamentary career consequently ended in ignominy, and it would be both shameful and dangerous to our democracy for anyone ever to encourage a comeback.

The lesson to be drawn is that there are many challenges to meet in both the short and longer term if the pitiful inadequacy of ministerial accountability and its consequent corrosive effect on parliamentary democracy are to be corrected. Yet more urgent cause for Parliament to take back control.

Chapter 8
The impartiality of the civil service

Witch-hunts against civil servants who are not 'fellow-travellers'.

- Commission a review of the practical working of the Constitutional Reform & Governance Act 2010 and involve all levels of the civil service and their representatives in the exercise.
- Only the Cabinet Secretary to be empowered to remove a Permanent Secretary from a department – and only on performance or disciplinary grounds, which can be tested in law.
- Clarify that the role of spads is to advise ministers with no power to instruct or direct civil servants.

Britain's tradition of an impartial and professional civil service traces its roots back at least to the Northcote-Trevelyan Report of 1854, commissioned by Gladstone as Chancellor, which is generally regarded as the founding document of the British civil service.

Drawing inspiration from Imperial China's ancient tradition of examinations, it recommended their use so that entry to the civil service be solely on merit. Peter Hennessy credits that report with *"enshrining the service with the core values of integrity, propriety, objectivity and appointment on merit, able to transfer its loyalty and expertise from one elected government to the next."*

One could go back further to Burke and Fox seeking admirably in the 1780s to reduce the influence of the executive and monarchy in the House of Commons, not least through the abolition of numerous offices and sinecures.

Yet this tradition of impartiality and political neutrality – for so long the envy of the democratic world – has in recent years come under attack from autocratic and high-handed ministers like never before (at least since the era Burke and Fox sought to consign to history).

Michael Gove, generally perceived as the most erudite of current – indeed recent – cabinet ministers, notoriously said during the Brexit referendum campaign that Britain had 'had enough of experts'. Regrettably his maxim has been keenly adopted by some of his colleagues less equipped to deploy it discerningly. Since the national schism of 2016, Conservative administrations have executed something of a witch-hunt against top civil servants whom they do not consider to be sufficiently enthusiastic fellow-travellers on their ideological path.

Ideological witch-hunts

In 2017, Britain's widely-respected Permanent Representative to the EU, Sir Ivan Rogers, was hounded out by hostile Brexiteers in government because he was delivering unpalatable truths about the Brexit process, including warnings about how long it would all take (amply vindicated by subsequent events). John Redwood welcomed his departure, moaning that Sir Ivan saw Brexit as "*difficult and long-winded*", and saying the new ambassador should be someone "*who thinks it's straightforward*".

Nigel Farage said: "*The Foreign Office needs a complete clear-out.*" By contrast, George Osborne said Sir Ivan was a *"perceptive, pragmatic and patriotic public servant,"* while former Treasury Permanent Secretary (Lord) Nick Macpherson said his departure marked a *"wilful and total destruction"* of EU expertise in Whitehall.

The Brexit process ended up being led by David Frost, who appeared to make a comprehensive mess of it, then went on to show his true colours by becoming a Conservative peer and minister, resigning after just nine months because he thought even Boris Johnson's government wasn't right wing enough.

During the Conservative leadership contest in summer 2022, he even seemed, bizarrely, to appoint himself as arbiter of who could carry the true right-wing flame and faith, despite never having been elected to anything.

In just six months in 2020, the Johnson government ran six permanent secretaries out of town. Sir Philip Rutnam, a career civil servant, was forced out of his post at the Home Office and began legal proceedings against the department, alleging bullying. In a hastily arranged press conference in his garden, Rutnam told the media that he had become the target of a *"vicious and orchestrated campaign"* against him, that he was run out of his job for defending his staff, and was suing the government under whistleblowing laws. The government ended up paying him £340,000 plus legal costs.

In a novel twist on the concept of ministerial account-ability, No 10 removed Jonathan Slater from Education in the wake of the (Covid-19) exams fiasco and Sally Collier departed as chief executive of the regulator Ofqual, while the perennially hopeless Gavin Williamson remained as Education Secretary.

In June 2020, Mark Sedwill departed as cabinet

secretary and head of the civil service after he became the target for hostile and anonymous politicised briefings and toxic social media.

The Foreign and Commonwealth Office lost Sir Simon McDonald, who served seven Prime Ministers from Thatcher to Johnson, and later said Johnson was the worst Prime Minister he worked under, although *"always charming to deal with.... charismatic but chaotic."* The Ministry of Justice's Sir Richard Heaton left as a casualty of Dominic Cummings's 'overhaul' of senior Whitehall jobs. Dame Melanie Dawes at Housing, Communities & Local Government at least enjoyed the old-fashioned exit of promotion sideways (at best) to become chief executive of Ofcom. Most victims of the purges saw their civil service careers prematurely ended whilst at the top of their game.

Worse to follow

If the Johnson government appeared to be the very nadir of decent public administration, worse was to come. Liz Truss and her Chancellor Kwasi Kwarteng, with breath-taking arrogance, dismissed immediately on taking office the Treasury Permanent Secretary Tom Scholar, and then just days later delivered a mini-Budget which had not even been costed by officials, only to seem surprised that it triggered a market collapse and put millions of pounds onto the nation's mortgage bills. The only redeeming virtue of that administration was that it ended after just 49 days, though the public will continue to feel the pain of her blundering for a long while to come.

Despite the exit of so many top officials causing a huge reservoir of senior talent being lost to the civil service, their ministerial counterparts – widely acknowledged to be the least cerebral or accomplished in generations – remained in post.

Compounding all of this came serial complaints against firstly Priti Patel and later Dominic Raab for bullying civil servants. The cases against Patel were investigated and upheld by Sir Alex Allan, Adviser on Ministerial Standards, which should under the terms of the Ministerial Code have occasioned her departure. Instead, Johnson overruled the finding causing Sir Alex, rather than the miscreant, to quit.

Eight cases against Raab involving 24 civil servants were referred for investigation and, on account of Sunak's sloth in appointing a new adviser, the lawyer Adam Tolley KC had to investigate incidents covering Raab's stints as Brexit Secretary, Foreign Secretary and Justice Secretary/Deputy PM. Tolley found that "*a description of bullying had been met,*" amounting to "*abuse or misuse of power*" *when Raab was Foreign Secretary. And he acted in a* "*manner which was intimidating*" and "*aggressive*" towards Ministry of Justice officials, though he "*did not intend by the conduct described to upset or humiliate... nor target anyone.*"

Raab resigned and said he will also stand down at the next election, but it remains a mystery why Sunak appointed him in the first place, having taken office pledging pieties about restoring "*integrity, professionalism and accountability,*" given how widely the allegations were known around Whitehall.

Thatcher recast the role of civil servants

The civil service historically operated around the principle that civil servants advise but ministers decide – and so take responsibility when things go wrong. In *The Blunders of our Governments* (2013), Anthony King and Ivor Crewe trace the change in relations between ministers and civil servants back to Thatcher, noting that she liked proactive, ideological ministers who took firm control of their departments.

In so doing, she recast the role of civil servants. They were no longer there to offer impartial advice as equal partners in the delivery of good government, but were to be enthusiastic deliverers of whatever policy ideas or ideology her strong-minded ministers brought to the table.

Alongside this has come the rise of politically-appointed special advisers (spads) to new heights of power. Under Dominic Cummings at No 10, he and other spads sat at the very centre of government, seeming routinely to be giving orders to civil servants and actually removing them if not deemed to be politically helpful. (Even Alistair Campbell – and his alter ego as the fictional 'Malcolm Tucker' – while he may have threatened this, for example over the sexing up of the Iraq 'dodgy dossier', does not seem on any available evidence to have actually fired anyone.)

The climate of fear this created means that, even when axed, senior mandarins have been replaced by other career civil servants, the new appointees have arrived knowing from the outset that it can be very costly not to tell ministers and their henchmen just exactly what they want to hear.

Contempt for checks and balances

What all of this illustrates is the fact that governments arrive in office, get their feet under the desks, and then start treating with contempt everyone whose duty it is to provide any sort of checks and balances, be this Parliament, civil servants, devolved and local government, the media – particularly the BBC (as it is funded by the public) - the monarchy (as held in the Prorogation judgement), the EU (Brexit) and the law (plans to reduce the scope of Judicial Review and threats to recast the UK Human Rights Act and withdraw from the European Convention on Human Rights).

Such megalomania is then exacerbated when overlaid with the mindset of a certain type of Conservative that they are born with a divine right to rule, although it was unseemly enough when our flawed electoral system gave huge parliamentary majorities to 'New Labour', distorting the will of the public.

In recent years a number of Conservative ministers and former ministers have taken to blaming 'the Blob' – a byword for the civil service – in their frustration over their own failing policies, most notably Brexit. In July 2023 Simon Case, the country's most senior civil servant, giving evidence to the Commons public administration committee, said ministers who attack the civil service as 'the Blob' are guilty of using 'dehumanising' language and 'self-defeating cowardice'. He went on to say that he had witnessed an "*increased number of attacks*" on the civil service, which had "*undoubtedly undermined the good functioning of government*," and observed that the last five years (spanning the time of Boris Johnson, Liz Truss and Rishi Sunak) had seen a "*deterioration in relations between officials and politicians.*"

Any fair-minded reader will agree that there is now something fundamentally broken in the relationship between government and civil service, but two questions arise. First, how this relates to our central theme of the relationship between Parliament and government; and secondly, what can be done about it?

An impartial and politically neutral civil service is a key factor in the delicate power balance between Parliament and government. Unlike most other democracies, Britain is unusual in keeping the civil service as the domain of the party in power and Parliament having little access behind its doors. Direct enquiries to civil servants from MPs – particularly in opposition – sometimes trigger indignation from ministers, along the lines of *"I gather you have been worrying my sheep; in future direct all enquiries to me."*

Heading towards the American system of political appointees

With tensions mounting and the annual survey of civil servants at the end of 2022 showing morale as the worst it has ever been, it is possible that the senior civil service will never be the same again. There is a sense of the UK heading towards the American model, where the most senior positions are filled with political appointees brought in by each new government.

Parliament must, however, be able to trust the answers, evidence and information both prepared and supplied by civil servants, which would risk becoming all but impossible if the civil service were politicised. As an example, the UK Statistics Authority has investigated repeated complaints of ministers misrepresenting data to give false impressions, and if officials were similarly politically motivated to distort facts, we would descend into a Trumpian morass of 'alternative facts'.

If we were to emulate our American counterparts, it could be anticipated that Parliament would demand much greater powers, including for certain American-style approval processes right down through the tree of political appointments, taking ages at the start of each Parliament. They might also reasonably take powers to arraign such post-holders, penalise and if needs be remove them. The shift in our political culture would be seismic.

If we are to avoid such a radical departure, then the current system needs urgent repair. We have a well-established Civil Service Code, given a statutory footing in 2010, which demands of civil servants:

• *Integrity* – putting the obligations of public service above your own personal interests.

• *Honesty* – being truthful and open.

• *Objectivity* – basing your advice and decisions on rigorous analysis of the evidence.

• *Impartiality* – serving equally well governments of different political persuasions, objectively.

Rescuing and improving our British system

The Civil Service Commission guidance also spells out what individuals should do if they believe they are being required to act in a way which conflicts with the code – either through line managers, nominated officers, whistleblowing procedures, or even to the Commission itself.

The only improvement should be a specialist office set up and ready to investigate pressure being applied on or over the four core values.

By contrast, as we have observed elsewhere, the Ministerial Code has more obvious shortcomings. It does say: *"Ministers must uphold the political impartiality of the civil service, and not ask civil servants to act in any way*

which would conflict with the Civil Service Code.... [and]....
ministers should be professional in their working
relationships with the civil service and treat all those with
whom they come into contact with consideration and
respect."

But that code lacks satisfactory enforcement mechanisms, with the Independent Adviser role having been exposed as unfit for purpose and the Prime Minister absurdly acting as gatekeeper over what issues are to be investigated, and even more absurdly over what the outcome will be.

The Constitutional Reform & Governance Act 2010 (CRAG) was an extremely belated attempt, more than a century after Northcote-Trevelyan, to give a statutory basis for a fully professional but impartial civil service. It enjoyed wide support in parliament. It is hard to know whether it simply a coincidence that disreputable politicians have caused the worst relapse in our culture to happen since then, but at the very least there seems a need for a comprehensive review of the relevant parts of that Act.

If these particular Augean stables are to be cleaned out, only Parliament can do it. The obvious solution is a statutory Ministerial Code with an open, independent and responsive enforcement mechanism.

If not, the palpable shift in power will take root and become irreversible (perhaps it is already). Not only the senior civil servants who are supposed to offer impartial advice and 'speak truth to power' are losers, but so too are public discourse, democratic government and the public interest.

Chapter 9
Reform of the upper House
We have been waiting since 1911 for a 'second chamber constituted on a popular basis'.

- Build on the widely-backed 2012 House of Lords Reform Bill as the starting template for change.
- Adopt its largely or wholly elected second chamber of around 450 members, directly elected by STV in multi-member regional (English) and national (Scotland, Wales and Northern Ireland) constituencies.
- Elect 1/3 of the members every 4-5 years, so that MPs always have a more powerful recent mandate.
- Non-renewable 12 or 15-year terms would give a longer outlook, with more independence from parties.

On 10 July 2012, the House of Commons gave the second reading of the coalition government's House of Lords Reform Bill an enormous 338-vote majority. Conservative MPs backed it by 193 to 89 votes, Labour by 202 to 26, and Liberal Democrats by 53 to 0.

This unprecedented victory for a major constitutional bill had its roots in a long, complicated and very detailed genesis. A century before, in 1911, in the wake of the crisis caused by peers resisting very modest taxation proposals from Lloyd George, Parliament had approved limits on the Lords' powers of delay and defiance. Membership remained by appointment and aristocratic inheritance.

Even so, the Parliament Act's long title stated boldly: "*It is intended to substitute for the House of Lords as it at present exists a second chamber constituted on a popular instead of hereditary basis, but such substitution cannot be immediately brought into operation."*

Now, 112 years later, the word 'immediately' sounds laughable.

In the intervening years, significant incremental changes to the composition of the House have been agreed. In 1958, appointed life peers brought in many more women (only a tiny number of Scottish hereditary titles could previously be inherited by women). The incoming Blair government in 1998 tried to alter the balance by limiting the number of hereditary peers, but gave in to a compromise proposal which permitted their 'temporary' survival through cumbersome and farcical by-elections. Labour ministers kicked this into long grass, saying it would continue only until more comprehensive democratic reform was implemented.

Cross-party discussions

Years of cross-party discussion resulted. A Royal Commission, chaired by Lord Wakeham, reported in 2000. Its recommendation of a very modest minority of elected members (between 12 and 35 per cent) was not well received.

The Labour Party manifesto of 2001 committed the returned government to a *"more representative and democratic"* second chamber. Yet its subsequent white paper was very cautious, proposing just 20 per cent elected, despite opinion polls showing 78 per cent public support for a majority being elected.

The government decided to back off. Instead, a joint

committee of MPs and peers was tasked to review all the issues in 2002-03. Failing to agree on a precise recommendation, it came up with seven options, ranging from all-appointed membership to all-elected.

The Leader of the Commons, Robin Cook, was persuaded – against his better judgement – to offer each of these for separate individual votes in each House in February 2003. All too predictably, none of them gained a majority in the Commons, although an 80 per cent elected second chamber only lost by 284 to 281 votes. Peers, also predictably if depressingly, voted 335 to 110 for their own survival as appointees.

Into this apparent impasse stepped a cross-party group of MPs – Ken Clarke and Sir George Young from the Conservatives, Robin Cook (after his resignation from the government over Iraq) and Tony Wright from Labour, and Paul Tyler from the Liberal Democrats. Their resulting 2005 report *Reforming the House of Lords – Breaking the Deadlock* set out in detail a plan to replace the existing House over time with 80 per cent elected by a proportional system in the nations and regions of the UK.

A draft Second Chamber of Parliament Bill was attached. Twenty-two other prominent MPs, and six leading peers - from all three major parties - gave general support to their proposals.

During the 2005-10 Parliament, a renewed attempt at cross-party consensus was made, significantly in the context of the Governance of Britain policy reset under Gordon Brown. Jack Straw convened a high-powered group to work up details, and published a white paper with its support in 2008, continuing along similar lines to the 2005 report.

The coalition government's 2012 bill

The incoming coalition government was therefore able to build on a decade of co-operative analysis and drafting in preparing its own white paper, published in May 2011. Led by Deputy Prime Minister Nick Clegg, but with the specific daily attention of Conservative high-flyer Mark Harper, this exercise had the full endorsement of Prime Minister David Cameron and his cabinet.

Their white paper, submitted to a joint committee of MPs and peers in July 2011, incorporated much of the previous work. After some 30 meetings, spread over many months, the committee published its report in April 2012, with a majority of 13 to 9 (9 MPs and 4 peers versus 1 MP, 7 peers and 1 bishop) endorsing the proposal that "*the reformed chamber of the legislature should have an elected mandate.*"

The Cameron government's 2012 bill drew almost exclusively on that joint committee report. While reiterating the 'primacy' of the Commons, it underpinned this by providing for a new chamber of 80 per cent elected members, with one third of the elected membership being elected every five years, thereby ensuring that MPs always had a more powerful and recent collective mandate.

The elections would be by Single Transferable Vote (STV) in multi-member regional (English) and national (Scotland, Wales and Northern Ireland) constituencies. Over the transition period of three elections, membership would reduce to 450, calculated as the appropriate number to both serve the scrutiny process and enable its hybrid of elected and appointed members to include some part- as well as full-timers. A compromise was reached on the length of terms of service: non-renewable 15-year terms would give a longer outlook to members, compared to Commons members, with more independence from their parties who might otherwise try to exercise pressure over their re-selection.

Overall, the package was calculated to appeal to reformer MPs in all parties. And so it proved. Amongst the huge majority of Labour MPs who supported the bill on 10 July 2012 was Gordon Brown. Still, by 2022 and his Commission on the UK's Future, prepared for Keir Starmer, he surprisingly proposed to ignore the years of cross-party consensus and instead start from scratch with vague plans for consultation. He and Keir Starmer may have intended this to divert attention from pressure for electoral reform for the Commons, newly demanded by their 2022 party conference. If so, they were only partly successful.

Obstructions to progress

The unprecedented majority for the 2012 bill's second reading did not, sadly, ensure its progress. As soon as it appeared, the Labour opposition led by Ed Miliband resorted to obstruction, by objecting to every government offer on timing of the bill's consideration (to be agreed in a 'programme motion'). They were joined by a minority of Conservative rebels.

Ministers, led by Sir George Young, Leader of the House, appealed in vain for some Labour indication of what timing they <u>would</u> accept. No answer came. The official opposition, for whatever reason, refused to budge. Whether they simply wanted to cover up their own policy divisions, or expose the differences on the Conservative benches, or even get a personal hit on Nick Clegg was not clear. Perhaps it was all three.

In any case, these party games stopped progress in its tracks. Alongside the remarkable second reading victory, Sir George had to announce a retreat on his programme motion attempt before the Summer Recess. In September, the bill was effectively withdrawn. Since 2012, governments have only permitted legislation for very minor reforms, allowing retirement from the Lords, for example. The focus has instead moved onto appointments, their number and individual merit.

Controversial appointments

The nominal size of the House has been a persistent cause of controversy. At over 820 members, it exceeds the 650 of the Commons and almost all other legislative bodies in the world. The fact that even the most exciting issue typically only attracts votes from about 500 peers vividly underscores the absurdity of the position.

Lord (Norman) Fowler, as Lord Speaker, set up an inquiry under Lord (Terry) Burns in 2016 to seek solutions. That group's 2017 report recommended progress towards a maximum of 600 members, with a pragmatic central commitment from Prime Ministers that each new appointment would be dependent on two departures. Under Theresa May, this was informally agreed, and during her period in No 10 the total numbers did decline.

Boris Johnson's arrival put a stop to that. He refused to be bound by his predecessor's agreement. Up to his July 2022 resignation as party leader, he had nominated 35 Conservatives, and almost as many Labour, crossbench or non-aligned peers. By June 2021, the Burns Group was warning that this refusal of restraint was unsustainable.

They also reiterated the view that an end to the 1999 (essentially temporary) mechanism for replenishing hereditary peers by means of an esoteric process was long overdue.

Some Johnson nominations were very controversial. That of Evgeny Lebedev in July 2020 – apparently against the advice of the security services – still raises damning questions three years later. Perhaps even more damaging to the integrity of the whole appointment system was the eventual arrival of multi-millionaire Peter Cruddas in 2020, after he was blocked by the House of Lords Appointments Commission. He had resigned as Conservative Party Treasurer, amidst accusations of preferential access and appointments offered to the party's big donors. He himself donated £500,000 just days after his own elevation. Johnson, arrogant as ever, simply over-ruled the Commission.

From his departure as party leader in July 2022 until well into 2023, rumours of Johnson's planned 'resignation honours list' caused new controversy. It was even reported that he was told to insist on strict future adherence to the instructions of Conservative whips as they feared he might nominate characters of unacceptable independence. Suggestions that he might try to nominate between 30 and 50 staunch Brexiteers and party donors on those terms made even Conservatives apprehensive.

In the event, the long-delayed list proved even more controversial. Coinciding with his departure from the Commons, following the investigation into his repeated misleading over Partygate, Johnson's initial choice of potential legislators proved too much even for the Appointments Commission. One of those who did get through the process – Shaun Bailey – was identified as the guest of honour at the illicit Conservative HQ Jingle & Mingle lockdown party which appeared in a leaked video at precisely the moment of his nomination. Others seemed too close to the No. 10 party ethos to be appropriate.

Liz Truss seems to have no inhibitions. We are told that her intended nominations – like her ministerial appointments – are from her own faction in the party. Some of those were very controversial, and on peerages she shows no appetite for the previous self-discipline on numbers agreed by Theresa May. Her record speed in and out of No 10 didn't seem to blunt her enthusiasm for nomination of political cronies.

Damage to the reputation of Parliament

Whatever the size and nature of dissolution and resignation lists may do for the reputation of Parliament, they certainly do not encourage public confidence in the appointment system. According to the UCL Constitution Unit only 6 per cent of UK voters think the Prime Minister should have sole power to appoint peers.

Even staunch Conservative peer Professor Lord Norton of Louth – his party's top constitutional pundit – baulked at this cavalier attitude. His House of Lords (Peerage Nominations) Bill won a second reading in the Lords on 18 November 2022 with almost unanimous support, except (of course) from the minister. It would strengthen the independence of the Appointments Commission, putting it on a statutory basis, to prevent Prime Ministers from overruling its recommendations.

It attempted to restrain government from overloading the House with a majority of its supporters, and required commitment from nominees that they would turn up to work. Finally, party leaders would have to spell out how their nominees were chosen, to increase transparency. This bill is unlikely to progress as it overtly restricts Prime Ministerial patronage. But its authorship, and acceptance across the House, reawakens the whole reform issue.

The events of 2023 have surely driven a fatal nail into the current appointments process for part of our legislature: tinkering, in the absence of comprehensive democratic reform, is surely past its sale date.

Revisiting the 2012 bill
Meanwhile, a growing consensus outside Parliament has revived reform discussion. Responding to this, Keir Starmer, Gordon Brown and Andy Burnham are amongst the many to argue for a 'senate' elected to represent the nations and regions of the UK. How unfortunate that they couldn't persuade their Labour colleagues in 2012, when a bill could have achieved just that. By now, that outcome could have been well on the way to fruition.

We simply must not let the opportunity for action slip by again. Strengthening Parliament vis-à-vis the executive needs both Houses to have credibility as well as more effective mechanisms to ensure accountability. Without any democratic legitimacy, the second chamber will always be ultimately impotent, however well qualified its members.

What is to be done? Cautious commentators – taking a lead from Professor Meg Russell of UCL – seem inclined to recommend only laborious attrition, such as removing remaining hereditary peers, toughening appointment checks and abolishing the Prime Minister's diktat. Yet anyone reflecting on past attempts would soon realise that this could easily cause just as hopeless a parliamentary constipation as would a comprehensive reform package.

Diehards in the current House of Lords would occupy the last ditch, anticipating this as the thin end of the wedge. The various reform attempts from 1968 to 2012 saw rebel MPs willing to join forces with them to stymie even agreed compromise proposals.

Similarly, given all the other urgent structural reforms necessary to strengthen the UK constitution (not least those listed in this book), together with all the other social, economic and environmental priorities facing the new government, returning to square one would be absurd. Wasting time and ignoring all the careful consensual preparation of the last two decades would be the height of irresponsibility.

The obvious solution is to reintroduce the broadly supported 2012 bill, improve and amend it if necessary, removing both the taint of corruption and of illegitimacy that haunts the current anachronism. Only then will progress to the much-delayed promise from 1911 of a 'popular' basis for the second chamber of our legislature finally be on the way to being delivered.

Chapter 10

Standards in Public Life
Politics on sale to the highest bidder – even if Russian.

- Enact the CPSL's 2021 report Upholding Standards in Public Life with strong independent regulators.
- Enact the principles of the CSPL's 2011 report Political Party Finance, with limits on donations, reduced expenditure limits and a modest increase in the existing level of state funding.

"In the four countries of the United Kingdom, we take democracy for granted. We should not. If you look around the world, you will find it is in retreat in many countries and has been for 10 to 15 years or more. It looks like that is going to continue. The point is this: democracy is not inevitable. It can be undone step by step, action by action, and falsehood by falsehood. It needs to be protected at all times. If our law and our accepted conventions are ignored, it seems to me that we are on a very slippery slope that ends with pulling our constitution into shreds.

"What has been done in the last three years has damaged our country, at home and overseas, and damaged the reputation of Parliament as well. The blame for these lapses lies principally, but not only, with the Prime Minister. Many in his cabinet are culpable too, and so are those outside the cabinet who cheered him on. They were silent when they should have spoken out, and then they spoke out only when their silence became self-damaging.

"All of this can be corrected. The task for Parliament, the government and this committee will be to restore constitutional standards and protect from any further slippage against them. That is a very important issue not just for now, but for the future. Bad habits, if they become ingrained, become precedent. Precedent can carry bad habits on for a very long time, and should not be permitted to do so."

Sir John Major
Oral evidence to the Public Administration & Constitutional Affairs Committee, 12 July 2022.

The Committee on Standards in Public Life (CSPL) was set up by John Major as Prime Minister in 1996 – with widespread public and political support – in recognition of dwindling confidence and respect for ethical behaviour in Parliament, the civil service and all levels of government. It followed a period of intense media and public interest in 'sleaze'.

In 1997 the committee's first chairman, Lord Nolan, promoted the 'Seven Principles of Public Life': selflessness, integrity, objectivity, accountability, transparency, honesty, and leadership.

In November 2021, some 25 years after its creation, the CSPL published its final report on a review entitled *Upholding Standards in Public Life*, with an introduction by John Major. Its recommendations included a new description for the principle of leadership:

"Holders of public office should exhibit these principles in their own behaviour and treat others with respect. They should actively promote and robustly support the principles and challenge poor behaviour wherever it occurs."

It also proposed strengthened independence for the various regulators of standards, with explicit accountability to Parliament, rather than simply to ministers, through primary legislation. The roles of the Independent Adviser on Ministerial Standards, the Advisory Committee on Business Appointments and the House of Lords Appointments Committee should all be freed from government interference and given statutory protection.

"*The Ministerial Code should be a code of conduct of ethical standards for ministers, akin to MPs' and peers' codes of conduct, based on the Seven Principles of Public Life*," it also concluded.

The government's response – both in words and action – was less than enthusiastic. The current chair of the CSPL, the formidable former head of MI5, Lord Evans of Weardale, expressed frustration that the trend appeared to be at variance with the committee's analysis and recommendations.

Partisan patronage remains controversial. In one of his very last grubby acts as Prime Minister, Boris Johnson appointed Baroness (Simone) Finn to fill a CSPL vacancy. Since she had been a key member of the hierarchy in No 10 throughout the Partygate era as his deputy chief of staff, this was understandably interpreted as a dismissive gesture.

Liz Truss was also reported to have stated that she "*didn't need an ethics adviser*," just as the widespread tributes to the integrity of the late Queen were being expressed; there seemed to be little hope of a change of attitude from the new regime.

The growing influence of money in politics

Since its inception, the CSPL has been concerned at the growing influence of money in UK politics. The public perception that millions of pounds rather than millions of votes steered policy decisions was seen to be corrosive. All three major parties previously appeared to agree. Their 2010 election manifestos contained broadly similar commitments.

Conservative: *"The public are concerned about the influence of money in politics, whether it is from trade unions, individuals, or the lobbying industry. We will seek an agreement on a comprehensive package of reform that will encourage individual donations and include an across-the-board cap on donations. This will mark the end of the big donor era and the problems it has entailed."*

Labour: *"We believe that the funding of political parties must be reformed if the public is to regain trust in politics. Our starting point should be the Hayden Phillips proposals of 2008. We will seek to reopen discussions on party funding reform, with a clear understanding that any changes should only be made on the basis of cross-party agreement and widespread public support."*

Liberal Democrat: *"We will get big money out of politics by capping donations at £10,000 and limiting spending throughout the electoral cycle."*

The CSPL – optimistically – believed these commitments. In November 2011, it published its detailed recomendations in *Political Party Finance*, with limits on donations, reduced expenditure limits and a very modest increase in the existing level of state funding. To their continuing shame, all three party leaders, including Nick Clegg as the minister responsible, and the coalition cabinet, shelved the report.

Their excuse was that the public would not wear any increase in taxpayer support for politics at a time of tight squeeze on household incomes. Conveniently, they made no effort to explain that a healthier democracy could be achieved for less than £1 per elector per year, nor even to admit that state funding of the parties already existed. Most significantly, David Cameron was able quietly to ditch his manifesto commitment to 'end the big donor era' and capitalised on this to huge advantage in the 2015 election.

A draft backbench cross-party bill, published in April 2013, sought to incorporate the main features of the CSPL scheme, while responding to the expressed concerns. It even itemised considerable savings in other electoral expenditure to enable the restrictions on donations to be offset by limited additional state funding. No Conservative government has even been prepared to consult further on this issue.

In the following decade the CSPL regularly returned to this failure, but with no confidence that action would follow. In July 2021, it limited itself in its report *Regulating Election Finance* to "practical proposals that seek to modernise and reform aspects of the regime," without daring to return to the core anti-democratic elements of big money influence.

Even its recommendations for *"tightening the requirement to identify the true source of donations and reduce the potential for foreign money to influence UK elections,"* did not find favour with the Johnson administration. With the lingering rumours of Russian involvement in the EU referendum, and Russian donations to individual MPs and parties, this serious concern from a public watchdog might have seemed urgent – but it was ignored.

By November 2021, the CSPL report *Upholding Standards in Public Life,* while acknowledging that public perception of ethical standards was influenced by the big money issue, expressed no hope of reform.

Transparency in public life

Meanwhile, its most rigorous and far-reaching analysis concerned transparency. But would its recommendations make a substantial difference? For example, its proposed improvements to the recording and publishing of lobbying activity echoed frequent attempts to strengthen the 2014 Transparency Act. Worthy perhaps, but in themselves hardly enough.

In parallel, a challenge by the Open Democracy campaign achieved a judicial ruling against the Cabinet Office's secretive 'clearing house', which was blacklisting Freedom of Information (FoI) requests from journalists. The Public Administration & Constitutional Affairs Committee had branded this as a *"slide away from transparency,"* with *"evidence of poor FoI administration in the Cabinet Office and across government which appears to be inconsistent with the spirit and principles of the FoI Act."* Ministers and civil servants were judged to view the 2000 FoI legislation as a hindrance to Whitehall, with Michael Gove dismissing complaints of obstruction as *"tendentious and ridiculous."*

Transparency is only effective if the public can rely on impartial, attentive and inquisitive media. In her Mac-Taggart Memorial Lecture at the August 2022 Edinburgh International Television Festival, the distinguished broad-caster Emily Maitlis was forthright:

"Facts are getting lost, constitutional norms trashed, claims frequently unchallenged... sections of both the BBC and government-supporting newspapers appear to go into an automatic crouch position whenever the Brexit issue looms large .... It feels like a conspiracy against British people."

116

Journalists are reluctant to discuss the impact of Brexit, she said, "*in case they get labelled pessimistic, anti-populist, or worse still, above all, unpatriotic.*"

Comment on her analysis tended to concentrate on two specifics: the BBC failure to stand up to No. 10 pressure, and the impact of a prominent Conservative appointment in the BBC hierarchy to continue that pressure. Her much wider and more substantial criticism of media failure was – unsurprisingly – less emphasised.

The BBC itself got away with a lame statement that it "*places the highest value on due impartiality and accuracy and we apply these principles to our reporting on all issues.*"

All the modest improvements suggested in *Upholding Standards in Public Life,* including mechanisms to enhance transparency, will be of little value if the dire situation so vividly described by Emily Maitlis continues after the end of the current government.

Follow the money

Meanwhile, the traditional advice of the seasoned investigative journalist – 'follow the money' – remains as relevant as ever. Scarcely a day goes by without a connection being made between a proposed tax break and party donations, or financial support for a MP or would-be PM and preferment, or regular donations and award of contracts.

The CSPL recommended that a blatant loophole in the regulation of political funding – by so called 'unincorporated associations' – must be blocked. In July 2023, Michael Gove refused to act. It is calculated that some £14 million of political donations have escaped scrutiny and control by this route since 2015. The CSPL described them as "*a route for foreign money to influence UK elections*".

Whenever a large political donation is made the question should be asked, "what is the donor expecting in return?" Father and son Lebedev have not been the only Russians to invest vast sums in UK politics, and especially in the Conservatives. What for? When new lobbying legislation was going through Parliament in 2014, David Cameron is reported to have quoted "*sunlight is the best disinfectant.*"

In yet another example of this, just as the public were grappling with new reports about Boris Johnson taking financial advice and assistance from his nominee for the BBC chairmanship in getting an £800,000 loan, and about Nadhim Zahawi's millions of pounds in tax liability, the CSPL had more to say. With consummate timing, on 24 January 2023, the committee's chairman, Lord Evans, wrote to political and other public body leaders emphasising the vital importance of a 'robust ethical culture'.

His questions to them covered such issues as leading by example, encouraging a 'speak up' culture and challenging 'behaviour that is not consistent with the Principles of Public Life'. Within the week, Zahawi had finally been sacked by the Prime Minister, who had claimed to be embracing just such an improved ethical approach on entering No. 10. At the time of writing, the evidence for this claim is negligible at best. Indeed the government has just resisted a number of improvements recommended by the CSPL and Institute for Government.

There is a real danger that the more the light shines on wrong-doing, the more it will fuel greater public disgust

118

and disenchantment unless real reforms, along the lines recommended by the CSPL, by us here, and by many others including the Electoral Commission, follows swiftly in its wake.

Conclusion

"The programme of the Conservative Party is to
maintain the constitution of the country."
Benjamin Disraeli, 1872

How his successors have turned that upside down and
laughed at his naïveté!

The effect of a series of recent insidious changes to the
UK constitutional settlement has been a common subject
of comment in the last year. A wide variety of politicians
(from John Major to Gordon Brown), respected academics
(such as the UCL Constitution Unit, and Professor Tim
Bale), think tanks (for example the Institute for Government, and the Hansard Society), pressure groups (like
Make Votes Matter, and Open Democracy), journalists
(Andrew Rawnsley, Matthew Parris) and most significantly
the Electoral Commission and Committee on Standards in
Public Life, have all raised profound concerns.

Yet there have been few attempts to collate and assess
the total impact. We cannot claim to have achieved the
definitive, comprehensive and cumulative assessment, but
we hope to have demonstrated the common themes which
should demand attention inside Parliament – and start a
political discourse.

Nor do we aspire to provide remedies for all the
problems identified. Others will, for example, promote the
abolition of First-The-Post-Post as a relic of a different
electoral era, in favour of a proportional voting system for
the House of Commons. This is the position of the Labour

Party conference, and it may yet arrive in their party manifesto for the coming general election, but of course it holds little appeal for power-hungry Conservatives.

Where we do detect broad agreement, across a surprising range of political opinion, is in an awareness that the Johnson government promoted or permitted a damaging trend of undermining our fragile constitution, which his successor has not shown any sign of reversing. Indeed, without the particular challenges of Covid, Rishi Sunak has even less excuse for some of the short cuts he has taken since Johnson left office. As an example, he has chosen wilfully and knowingly to double down on the dilution of the Ministerial Code.

Some may seek justification by suggesting that the Labour governments of Blair and Brown started this trend. Perhaps, but two wrongs do not make a right.

We are promoting the strong case for a rigorous and detailed re-examination of the constitutional constraints that Parliament can and should exercise on every government. This has been made even more urgent as a result of events during the Johnson reign, the chaos of the ensuing Truss turmoil and the ineffectual approach to these crucial matters which we have seen from Rishi Sunak, however calm and intelligent he may be in comparison to his two predecessors.

In their magisterial academic study, *The Parliamentary Battle Over Brexit* (OUP 2023), Meg Russell and Lisa James of the Constitutional Unit at UCL, summed up as follows: "*A saga that began with demands to enhance the sovereignty of parliament gradually developed into one where parliament was vilified.*"

Is there a public consensus that the threat of 'elective

dictatorship' is real and must be reversed? Not yet. Even so, informed opinion, combined with widespread disillusion and detachment from political activity, is creating a growing appetite for reform.

There is a body of evidence, most recently and effectively brought together by the Institute for Government and the UCL Constitution Unit, that these issues must be addressed if our parliamentary democracy is to survive and thrive in the 21st century. Their joint July 2023 report *Rebuilding and Renewing the Constitution: Options for Reform* may at first seem over-cautious, but as the authors expand on remedies there is no doubt of the severity of the challenges they are seeking to address.

Unless Parliament can be enabled to *take back control* from the executive, and prove itself to have the courage and strength of will to do so, the United Kingdom will fast descend the slippery slope to the 'elective dictatorship' about which we were so saliently and powerfully warned by Lord Hailsham – a true Conservative if ever there was one – nearly 50 years ago.

Appendix

Lord Hailsham
Elective Dictatorship
The Richard Dimbleby Lecture, 1976

Library of the House of Lords
from
Hailsham
1976

Lord Hailsham's Richard Dimbleby Lecture
Broadcast on Thursday 14 October 1976
© Lord Hailsham 1976

Reproduced here by kind permission of the
current Lord Hailsham

THIS LECTURE IS NAMED AFTER RICHARD DIMBLEBY, a man of patriotism and integrity and one of the most famous broadcasters in the world. I am proud to have been asked this year to deliver it in honour of his memory.

I have called it 'Elective Dictatorship'. You may think that a strange name. You may think it all the stranger when I tell you that I mean our own system of government which we have evolved throughout the centuries and which we are apt to think of as the best and most democratic in the world.

Now please do not misunderstand me. I am as proud of our country and its institutions as anyone. For seven hundred years we have been governed by one sovereign body consisting of the Queen, Lords, and Commons, in Parliament assembled.

It has served us well. We are rightly proud of its achievements. For century after century, it has seen us safely through one change after another, from medieval monarchy to modem democracy. Under it, in our own time, we have survived and been victorious in two immense world wars, largely because of the very qualities I am going to criticise. Even more strikingly, it is surely due to its unique combination of flexibility and authority that - for more than three hundred years - we have managed to live together as a nation in periods of constant change without the searing experience of violent revolution or civil war.

These are formidable and unique achievements. They fully justify our pride. They make it incumbent upon all of us to discuss potential changes in a spirit of humility and caution. Above all I would wish us to remember that our constitution has one advantage of priceless value; its immemorial antiquity which, with its power of continuous growth, gives a prestige and mystique not shared by any other nation in the world.

All the same, I think the time has come to take stock and to recognise how far this nation, supposedly dedicated to freedom under law, has moved towards a totalitarianism which can only be altered by a systematic and radical overhaul of our constitution.

We are sometimes unaware that our constitution is unique. There is nothing quite like it, even among nations to whom we have given independence. They believe of course that they have inherited the so-called Westminster model.

In fact, the Westminster model is something which we have seldom or never exported, and, if we had tried to do so, I doubt whether any nation would have been prepared to accept it. The point is not that all other nations have what is called a written constitution in the literal sense. After all, much of our own is in writing and much more could be reduced to writing if we wished without making any appreciable change.

No, the point is that the powers of our own Parliament are absolute and unlimited. In this we are almost alone. All other free nations impose limitations on their representative assemblies. We impose none on ours. Parliament can take away a man's liberty or his life without trial, and in past centuries has actually done so. It can prolong its own life, and in our own time has done so twice, quite properly, during each of two world wars.

No doubt, in recent times, Parliament has not abused its powers in these ways. Nonetheless, the point which I make to you this evening is that as a result of the changes in its operation and structure, the absence of any legal limitation on the powers of Parliament has become unacceptable. The questions which I desire to leave for your consideration are first, whether the time has not come to end or modify this legal theory, and, secondly, whether and how it is possible to do so.

Of course, this doctrine of the absolute sovereignty of Parliament has been fully recognised for very many years. Judges may pass judgement on the acts of ministers, as they recently have done in the Tameside dispute and in the arguments about the Laker Skytrain or the payment of sewerage rates.

To this extent the rule of law prevails here as in other free countries. But once the courts are confronted with an Act of Parliament, all they can do is to ascertain its meaning if they can and then apply it as justly and mercifully as the language of the law permits. So, of the two pillars of our constitution, the rule of law and the sovereignty of Parliament, it is the sovereignty of Parliament which is paramount in every case.

The limitations on its power are only political and moral. They are found in the consciences of members, in the necessity for periodical elections, and in the so-called checks and balances inherent in the composition, structure and practice of Parliament itself.

Only a revolution, bloody or peacefully contrived, can put an end to the situation which I have just described. We live under an elective dictatorship, absolute in theory, if hitherto thought tolerable in practice. How far it is still tolerable is the question which I wish to raise for discussion tonight.

A good deal of water has flowed under Westminster

Bridge since the sovereignty of Parliament was first established, and almost every drop of it has flowed in one direction, an enhancement of the actual use of its powers. To begin with, there has been a continuous enlargement of the scale and range of government itself. Then, there has been a change in the relative influence of the different elements in the Parliamentary machine, so as to place all the effective power. in the hands of one of them; in other words, to remove the checks and balances which in practice prevented a use. So, both sets of changes have operated on one another to increase the extent to which elective dictatorship is a fact and not just a lawyer's theory.

Until comparatively recently, Parliament consisted of two effective chambers. Now for most practical purposes it consists of one. Until recently, the powers of government within Parliament were largely controlled either by the opposition, or by its own back-benchers. It is now largely in the hands of the government machine, so that the executive controls the legislature and not vice versa. Until recently debate and argument dominated the Parliamentary scene. Now it is the whips and the party caucus. More and more debate is becoming a ritual dance sometimes interspersed with cat calls.

Let me develop one or two of these points in greater detail. Consider first the scale and range of modern government. The powers of government may have been tolerable when exercised in the limited manner say of the Liberal government of 1911, or even the governments between the wars.

But the same powers may well have become intolerable to the ordinary man in 1976 by reason of the vast mass and detail of legislation, the range of its application, and the

127

weight of taxation which goes with it.

Consider two simple criteria, the mass of annual legislation, and the size of the annual budget. Before the First World War, the Liberal government, generally acknowledged to be one of the great reforming administrations of our time, was content to pass a single slim volume of legislation in a year. In 1911 it was not much more than 450 pages, and that was a heavy year. Between the wars, this had virtually doubled. For 1975, there will probably be three volumes, each of about a thousand pages, and each carrying with it an immense flow of subordinate legislation, amounting to about ten volumes of over a thousand pages each.

So that when at last they have got round to printing it all there will be over 13,000 pages of legislation for a single year. It must be remembered, moreover, that these changes are cumulative. Even after allowing for repeals and amendments, the 13,000 pages in 1975 represented a huge addition to the corpus of British law and that had already reached an all-time high. So, year by year there are substantially more and more complicated laws to obey.

Another example. When Gladstone was Prime Minister, he was able to spend about five months of the year at his country home in North Wales, planting his garden, and felling the oak trees, and presenting the chips to respectful delegations of liberal working men. Today, if a Prime Minister takes time off to spend a weekend on the water on his yacht, there is an immediate outcry that he is only working part-time, as if the quality of his statesmanship was a direct result of the quantity of his output.

Then look at the budget. I suppose that at the turn of the century it could be expected never to amount to more than

£100 million pounds a year. It was already about £800 million when I was a young man. But by the end of the Second World War, we were spending twenty-five times as much as before the first. We are now spending about £50,000 million in the annual budget every year, and one in every four is borrowed. With local government expenditure, two-thirds of our income is spent by public authority.

Some of these changes were no doubt inevitable, and many others arguably desirable. But changes on this scale, even taking full account of the fall in the value of money, really represent alterations in the character of our institutions and not simply differences of degree.

At the same time, the checks and balances which controlled Parliament's use of its absolute powers have largely disappeared. Power has centralised itself more and more in the Commons, more and more on the government side of the House, more and more on the front benches, while the time allotted for debate of individual measures has become progressively less and less. As between the two Houses, the Commons have for many years been quite properly the dominant partner. They are elected. They control the finance and give the political colour to the government of the day. But the process has now developed to the point at which the sovereignty of Parliament has virtually become the sovereignty of the Commons.

I am not in the least suggesting that the House of Lords is useless or that its influence in modifying the details of legislation is without value, or that the effect of its debates in moulding instructed opinion is negligible. But I do say that it is not an effective balancing factor and cannot in practice control the advancing powers of the executive. Its

129

influence on government is far weaker than that of the senates in other countries like America, and is arguably less persuasive than a powerful leading article in *The Times*, or even a good edition of Panorama. So, the sovereignty of Parliament means more and more the sovereignty of the Commons House.

But how far are the Commons themselves really masters of their own House? Until fairly recently influence was fairly evenly balanced between government and opposition, and between front and hack benches. Today, the centre of gravity has moved decisively towards the government side of the house, and on that side to the members of the government itself.

The opposition is gradually being reduced to insignificance, and the government majority, where power resides, is itself becoming a tool in the hands of the cabinet. Back-benchers, where they show promise, are soon absorbed into the administration, and thus lose their powers of independent action. When Trollope wrote the Palliser novels a hundred years ago, parties were fluid, and government time less extensive. Even in 1906, a back-bench speech like F. E. Smith's maiden could make a considerable impact. But, in present conditions, the whole absolute powers of Parliament, except in a few matters like divorce or abortion, are wielded by the cabinet alone and sometimes by a relatively small group within the cabinet.

To begin with, the actual members of the government, with their Parliamentary private secretaries, are one of the largest and most disciplined single groups in the House. They number, I suppose, not much short of 130 out of the three hundred-odd members of the government party, and not one, so long as he retains his position, can exercise an independent judgement.

But, far more important than numbers, is the disproportionate influence of ministers in debate as the result of their possession of the civil service brief. The increasing complexity of public affairs makes meticulous research and specialisation almost indispensable for speaking in Parliament. The decreasing leisure and increasing economic pressures upon private members, few of whom live upon their Parliamentary salaries, make it more and more difficult to bring a minister to book. Even when he is wrong, he can usually make it look sufficiently as if he were right to get his own supporters into the lobby when the division bell rings.

I have been often enough both on the giving and the receiving end myself, and I must say frankly that, more often than not, right or wrong, it is the minister who wins the argument. So, the sovereignty of Parliament has increasingly become, in practice, the sovereignty of the Commons, and the sovereignty of the Commons has increasingly become the sovereignty of the government, which, in addition to its influence in Parliament, controls the party whips, the party machine and the civil service.

This means that what has always been an elective dictatorship in theory, but one in which the component parts operated in practice to control one another, has become a machine in which one of those parts has come to exercise a predominant influence over the rest. This has been accentuated by two further factors which I must now examine: the power of dissolution, and the doctrine of mandate and election manifesto.

The power of dissolution is of course no longer in the hands of the Crown. It is in the hands of the Prime

Minister. Have you noticed how seldom since the war a government in office has been unseated, even though the opinion polls have indicated during the greater part of those thirty years that the government has been less popular than the party in opposition? If we leave out 1945, there have been nine general elections since the war. Six resulted in a victory for government and, of the six, four were won with substantial, or increased majorities. Of the three general elections which resulted in a change, all three were won by the narrowest margin of seats, and either on a minority of votes, or the smallest possible majority over their nearest opponents.

Do you really believe that this is a coincidence? At the centre of the web sits the Prime Minister. There he sits with his hand on the lever of dissolution, which he is free to operate at any moment of his choice. In selecting that moment, he is able, with the Chancellor of the Exchequer, to manipulate the economy, so as to keep it possible for things to appear for a time better than they really are.

He operates the lever with his eyes fixed on the opinion polls, knowing that he is able to control in practice the loyalty of the party machine the moment his troops go into action. Criticism from below, however vocal before, is silenced until after polling day. Is it to be wondered at that he wins more often than he loses, and that, when he loses, his defeat is often the kind of surprise it was when Mr Wilson lost in June 1970 or Mr Heath in February 1974?

Thus, the dictatorship has proved more and more powerful, and more and more liable to perpetuate itself through the adroit manipulation of the economy, and the firm use of dissolution operated with a careful eye to by-elections and public opinion polls.

To these formidable factors I must now add the new, and to my mind wholly-unconstitutional, doctrines of mandate and manifesto. It is of course right and proper that when parties go to the country they should explain in broad language what they consider the situation requires in terms of general policy and what measures they would propose to carry out if entrusted with a majority in Parliament.

But in practice, while before the election the manifesto is written rather like the advertisement for a patent medicine, after the election it is treated as a pronouncement from Sinai with every jot and tittle of the unread and often unreadable document reverenced as Holy Writ. The actual situation with which a new government is confronted is often vastly different from what it was imagined to be in opposition, and the measures proposed in the manifesto often include the impossible, the irrelevant, and the inappropriate. But it is here that the doctrine of mandate takes over. However small the majority, however ill-advised the promises, however controversial the programme, the party activists, flushed with victory, insistently demand the redemption of all the pledges in the shortest possible time, and they are vociferously supported by the various pressure groups whose collective support has been won by the making of those pledges.

Since an election can be won on a small minority of votes - I will return to the electoral system later - it follows that the majority in the House of Commons is free to impose on the country a series of relatively unpopular measures, not related to current needs, using the whole powers of the elective dictatorship to carry them through.

In doing so it is not effectively controlled by a second chamber. It is not effectively opposed or criticised by an opposition or by back-benchers. Owing to the operation of the guillotine, and other regulations designed to curtail debate, much of the programme is often not discussed at all. It is idle to pretend that this system is rational, necessary, just, or even, to use an over-worked and not very illuminating word, democratic. That the programme often becomes unworkable long before the end of the Parliament and that its impracticability then results in a so-called U-turn is not really a mitigation of the system, let alone justification for it. It is simply a mark of the weakness of the system itself, and leads to general loss of confidence in the integrity of politicians.

Thus, it is a paradox of our system of government that at one and the same time it has become increasingly oppressive, decreasingly effective, and ever more manifestly absurd in its results.

It must not be supposed that these growing defects have passed wholly unnoticed or uncomplained of. On the contrary, there have been many criticisms and suggestions for· improvement. Scottish and Welsh nationalists want devolution. Others, particularly in England, demand a Bill of Rights, Electoral Reform, or reform of the House of Lords. The proposed remedies are different, though not necessarily inconsistent. I shall try to show that there is something in each, but not enough in any one, if taken by itself. The answer may be to incorporate elements from all.

If it were not for the fact that they aim at the destruction of the United Kingdom which, so far as I am concerned, is my country, I might have had most sympathy with the Nationalists. They alone wish to get rid of the whole incubus of absolute central authority, and manage their own affairs themselves on a more modest scale. So far, if they only wished to achieve their purpose within the ambit of a new federal constitution,

I can see nothing unreasonable about their aim. After all, nations as diverse as the Swiss, the Americans, the Canadians, the Australians and the Germans have all managed to achieve stability, efficiency, and prosperity on these very lines. So far as we are concerned, it is at least arguable that it was our failure to come to terms with federalism in any form which led to the severance of our connection with Ireland and therefore to the partition of the British Isles, with all the misery that that has entailed.

But I quarrel with the nationalists on a number of heads. In the first place, if devolution is seen as a step towards complete separation, I wholly reject it. Separation I regard as the destruction of my country, treason to the whole, treason to the separate parts, and worse still, treason to the Christian West of which we are all part and which now stands on the defensive against hostile forces determined to destroy everything that it stands for and all that it has contributed to human welfare.

In the second place, if devolution be right in Northern Ireland, (where I suppose it must ultimately be restored), and in Scotland and Wales, I cannot see that it is wrong for the Midlands, or the South West, North or South East of England. If devolution comes at all, sooner or later we must surely devise a structure under which the terms of membership of our nation must at least be roughly comparable whether we live in Manchester or Belfast, London or Cardiff, Norwich, Newcastle or Edinburgh, or rural Wales.

This is a much bigger undertaking than either the government or the nationalists seem to have realised, and although it is not impossible to achieve, a good deal more preliminary work has to be done.

In the third place, the real weakness of our constitution lies in the fact that it is an elective dictatorship and if we were to break up the United Kingdom into three or four little elective dictatorships, there can be no reason to believe that the peoples of Scotland, England, Wales and Northern Ireland would be any more content with their new masters than with their old.

Would we not be better served if we went on together on federal lines, without trampling in the dust the whole proud tradition of two hundred and fifty years? If we broke up the United Kingdom there can be no doubt that the several parts of these islands would be played off against one another by our various commercial and political rivals, that our common defences would be dismantled, and the contribution we jointly make to the common cause would be rendered negligible.

I for one do not wish to substitute a series of small and ineffective independent units in place of our existing historic association which, with all its defects, is nonetheless glorious in its acknowledged achievement.

By contrast with Wales and Scotland there is little sign of sufficient regional patriotism in England to give rise to demands for devolution. In England, therefore, the revolt against elective dictatorship has taken the form of demands for a Bill of Rights, Electoral Reform, or, less often, the reform of the second chamber.

The case for each of these is that it has become urgently necessary in the interest of liberty and the rule of law either to curb the legal powers of Parliament, or to recreate a system of checks and balances within it.

The advocates of a Bill of Rights are for limiting the powers. They argue, correctly, that every other civilised nation has imposed some limits upon its legislature, and has laws which make changes in the constitution either difficult or impossible.

In such cases the judges, or some special constitutional court, can strike down legislation which exceeds the bounds. But how can these limitations be made effective? Under our present arrangements, Parliament could always take away what it has given, by amending or repealing the bill. To this the advocates of the bill always reply that governments would be restrained by public opinion from doing that sort of thing.

I am afraid that I regard that view as extremely naive. I fully accept that a Bill of Rights might, in some cases, prevent interference with individual rights by some oversight in an ill-drafted Act of Parliament. But I do not accept that a party government of either colour would hesitate for a moment, with its main programme bills, to insert when it wished to do so, the necessary exempting words: 'Notwithstanding anything in the Bill of Rights or any other rule of law or statute to the contrary'.

I could almost compose the ministerial speech, of course of the most soothing and conciliatory kind, which would accompany such a section. Surely if it is to be worth the paper it is written on, a Bill of Rights must be part of a written constitution in which the powers of the legislature ate limited and subject to review by the courts. Otherwise, it will prove to be a pure exercise in public relations.

Even if I were wrong about this, I would be bound to

point out that a Bill of Rights could only solve a relatively small part of the problem. Infringement of individual rights is an important weakness of our elective dictatorship, but it is not the most important nor is it the one which occurs most frequently.

Should we not be more concerned with its remoteness, its over-centralisation, its capacity for giving control to relatively small minorities, and its dependence upon the enthusiasm of political caucuses and other outside bodies and pressure groups whose zeal, ideological bigotry and desire for irreversible change all too often outrun their discretion?

If, as I think, the powers of Parliament need restricting at all, the restrictions should not be limited to the protection of individual rights. I am sure that this is one reason why a large number of the English critics of elective dictatorship tum instead to electoral reform. This would create, so it is thought, within the lower House at least, a balance of parties which would eliminate extremism or at least control it.

But is this true? Has proportional representation had this effect in Northern Ireland? If anything, it seems to me to have increased polarisation, and deprived moderates, at least in the Unionist Party, even of such influence as they had before. Has it done so in European countries? I think not. On the whole it seems to have favoured the growth of communist, and even sometimes neo-fascist, groups.

So far as one can judge, in the scramble for second preference votes, or in the post-election horse trading, it tends to make moderates give concessions to extremists of their own persuasion rather than to moderates of the opposite viewpoint. Whatever the vices of our own system it at least tends to put the moderates in our large national parties in charge of their own extremists and that, to my mind, is a great merit.

In Scandinavia, on the other hand, these systems of voting have tended to keep a single party in power for periods of up to thirty or even forty years, and that at least is a form of elective dictatorship which, happily, we have not yet had here.

But the real weakness of electoral reform is that it does not touch the problem at its root. What is ultimately unfair about our present constitution is that it gives absolute power to the legislature when all reason and human experience tend to show that unlimited powers are intolerable. If this is right, no amount of tinkering with the method of electing the dictators will by itself deal with the evil of elective dictatorship. The best that can be hoped for is some mitigation of its effects.

I turn now to the House of Lords. I am quite sure that a legislature with two houses is desirable, though as with the other proposals, it would be quite wrong to think the existence of two houses would by itself be enough. It used to be said when I was young that a second chamber is either objectionable or unnecessary, unnecessary if it endorsed the decisions of the first, objectionable if it did not. I think this is wrong. By whatever means a single chamber is elected it is clear that it cannot be wholly representative for all purposes.

There will be areas, regions, interests not fully represented, whatever system of voting is adopted. This was recognised by the founding fathers of the United States. There, the Senate, on the whole, represents states, the House of Representatives numerical populations. In federal systems, this must clearly be desirable. What, however, is clear to me is that, useful and distinguished as the present House of Lords is, nothing further can be done to modify its present powers and composition. In the long run, it will be a question of abolition or replacement. Until then it is better to leave it alone. When the time comes, I shall be for replacement.

I have now come to the last stage of my journey. I have reached the conclusion that our constitution is wearing out. Its central defects are gradually coming to outweigh its merits, and its central defects consist in the absolute powers we confer on our sovereign body, and the concentration of those powers in an executive government formed out of one party which may not fairly represent the popular will.

I have come to think that, while there is much to be said for each of them, none of the reforms which I have examined is adequate by itself to redress the balance. I now owe it to you to give some indication of what might suffice and how it might be achieved.

I envisage nothing less than a written constitution for the United Kingdom and, by that, I mean one which limits the powers of Parliament and provides a means of enforcing these limitations either by political or legal means. This is the essence of the matter, and every other detailed suggestion that I make must be considered as tentative, and in comparison, unimportant.

I would myself visualise a Parliament divided into two chambers, each elected. The one, the Commons, would, as now, determine the political colour of the executive government and retain control of finance.

Preferably, in my view, it would be elected as now by

single member constituencies. The other, you might call it a senate, but I would prefer the old name, would, like the Senate of the United States, be elected to represent whole regions, and unlike that Senate, would be chosen by some system of proportional representation.

The powers of Parliament, so formed, would be limited both by law, and a system of checks and balances. Regions would have devolved assemblies, and the respective spheres of influence of these and of Parliament would be defined by law and policed by the ordinary courts.

There would be a Bill of Rights, equally entrenched, containing as a minimum the rights defined by the European convention to which we are already parties, and which can already be enforced against us by an international body.

Thus, Scotland, Wales and Northern Ireland would all obtain self-government in certain fields within the framework of a federal constitution of which the regions of England would also be separate and equal parts. The interests of regions, minorities and individuals would be safe-guarded by law, by the provision of a proportionately elected second chamber, and by the separate regional assemblies.

What we should have achieved is a recognisable version of the Westminster model modified so as to remove its disadvantages, as has already been done in Canada and Australia. The creation of such a constitution would clearly be a matter of years rather than months and you may well ask how it could be done.

Quite obviously, so long as we are content to muddle along in the good old British way, it cannot be done. But my own hunch is that circumstances, in the not-too-distant future, will force our hand and then we shall not be able to go on muddling along in the good old British way. If and when such a moment arrives, and, if possible, before then, here is my suggestion as to the stages by which we could hope to arrive at our destination.

In order to achieve it lawfully, we must make use of our existing institution, the Queen in Parliament. Seeing that Parliament is omnipotent it can in theory give us a new constitution as easily as it can nationalise the coal mines or join the Common Market. The question is not so much how we can get it, as how we could prevent it being taken away.

My own thought is that we should begin with an Act of summoning a constitutional convention, on the lines of those we hold before granting independence to a new member of the Commonwealth. This would have powers only to discuss and advise. Next, the government of the day would embody the outcome of the deliberations in a bill to be discussed in Parliament in the ordinary way.

Thirdly, if the bill were passed, it would be submitted to a referendum of the whole United Kingdom and, although this is controversial, if the separatists wished to opt out, the referendum would give them a chance to say so. This involves a risk of disaster, but one, I believe, which we would have to take.

Once the new constitution was adopted and in force it would be unalterable, except by a special procedure involving an Act of the newly constituted Parliament, perhaps passed by a qualifying majority, followed by another referendum.

You will see that I have said nothing, or virtually nothing, about the Crown. This is because it seems to me that our monarchy is the one part of our constitution which is working more or less as it is designed to do, to the great national benefit, and to the satisfaction of all but a few cranks. Obviously, its continuance would be incompatible with a communist state, and possibly, with a fully socialised one. But I do not contemplate either of these as a permanent, or even temporary, feature of the British political landscape.

Within the limitations of a mixed, free, and evolving community, I can see no rival to our present hereditary presidency (for that is what it is) except the so-called presidential system, in reality an elective monarchy, favoured by the United States and now by the Fifth Republic in France.

With great respect to the peoples of those two beloved countries, I can see nothing about their arrangements which would lead me to desire to import this feature of their constitutions into our own. It brings the headship of the state into the cockpit of party politics. It deprives the nation which adopts it of the glamour, prestige, and continuity which is one of the few remaining assets of our own society. A nation cannot survive by controversy alone; it needs cement, and that cement can in the long run only be afforded by tradition. Tradition needs symbols and our symbol is the Crown, guarding and forming a component part of our sovereign body, the Queen in a Parliament of two Houses, by which we have been ruled so gloriously and so long.

I would myself have wished to continue along these traditional lines unaltered even in the respects in which according to this lecture I have recommended or suggested change. I would not have made these recommendations if, at the end of a long life, if I had not seen unmistakable marks of disruption and dissolution.

My object is continuity and evolution, not change for its own sake. But my conviction remains that the best way of achieving continuity is by a thorough reconstruction of the fabric of our historic mansion. It is no longer wind or weatherproof. Nor are its foundations secure.

Check out other political books from the Real Press... at www.theRealPress.co.uk

FOURTH TO FIRST

HOW TO WIN A LOCAL ELECTION IN UNDER SIX MONTHS

FREYA SAMPSON
STEFFAN AQUARONE

SCANDAL

HOW HOMOSEXUALITY BECAME A CRIME

DAVID BOYLE

FREE DOWNLOAD

Get Remains of the Way for free...

☆☆☆☆☆

"Evocative and engaging mystery story set on the Pilgrim's Way with a political twist"

☆☆☆☆☆

"This book is a fine read...read this book a couple of months ago and it has stayed with me. Highly recommended

Printed in Great Britain
by Amazon